A Murderer's Country

Joyce Country, Galway during Ireland's Land War 1879-1882

Mary Lydon Simonsen

Quail Creek Publishing, LLC

©2017 Quail Creek Publishing, LLC

All rights reserved. No part of this publication may be reproduced, stored in a retrieval system, or transmitted in any form or by any means, electronic, mechanical, photocopying, recording or otherwise, without the prior written permission of the publisher.

Warning: The unauthorized reproduction or distribution of this copyrighted work is illegal. Criminal infringement, including infringement without monetary gain, is investigated by the FBI and is punishable by a fine of up to $250,000.

Thank you for buying an authorized edition of this book and for complying with copyright laws. In doing so, you are supporting writers by allowing them to continue to write by receiving earned compensation.

Printed in the United States of America
Published by Quail Creek Publishing, LLC
quailcreekpub@hotmail.com
Peoria, Arizona

Cover artwork: Eviction scene in the 1880s

ISBN 10: 978-0692910610
ISBN 13: 0692910611

Contents

Timeline

Introduction   i

Chapter

1	Vigilante Justice in Donegal	1
2	Years Leading Up to the Formation of the Land League	11
3	Mini-Famine: 1877-1879	14
4	The Land League	19
5	The Land War (1879-1882)	22
6	The Murder of Lord Mountmorres	25
7	Arthur Guinness, 1st Baron Ardilaun	45
	Map of Joyce Country	51
8	The Murders of Joseph and John Huddy	52
9	Maamtrasna Massacre and Phoenix Park Murders	65
	The Huddy Murder Trials – Cast of Characters	73
10	First Trial of Patrick Higgins	74
11	Second Trial of Patrick Higgins	89
12	Trial of Thomas Higgins	94
13	Trial of Michael Flynn	99
14	The Queen's Justice in Galway	108
15	Questions about the Huddy Murders	113
16	Aftermath – Maamtrasna Massacre	125
	Epilogue	131
	Notes	

Appendix

A	Maamtrasna Massacre
B	Maamtrasna Alliance
C	Parnell Commission
D	Lord Ardilaun after the Lough Mask Murders
E	Connemara

Acknowledgments

My thanks to those people in Counties Galway, Mayo, and Donegal, who provided local history that proved indispensible in writing this book, including Cloghbrack's postmistress, the docents at the Michael Davitt Museum in Straide, Ashford Castle, and Ballintubber Abbey, Mayo, and the Mayo Tourist Board in Cong, as well as a couple who were out for a walk on a beautiful afternoon in Donegal. I would especially like to thank my husband who served as my driver on Ireland's narrow and winding roads as well as a sounding board for my theories on the what, where, when, and how of these horrendous crimes.

This book came about as a result of my email correspondence with the late Dr. Joseph F. Lydon (1922-2011), a friend and neighbor of my father. "Minooka Joe" loved his grandmother, Mary Kerrigan; his hometown of Minooka, Pennsylvania; his church; and a good story. He insisted that every man and woman was a hero at his/her own funeral, and so it is with the memory of Mary Kerrigan.

Note to Readers

A Murderer's Country is written by an armchair historian who has spent much of her adult life reading Irish history and doing genealogical research on her family, many of whom immigrated to America from Joyce Country, Galway, and settled in Minooka and South Scranton, Pennsylvania. Members of my family were directly impacted by the events that took place in this book, and at least one witness to the Joseph and John Huddy murders moved to Minooka after the three men accused of the crime were convicted and hanged.

Most of the information included in the chapters on the murders of Lord Mountmorres and Joseph and John Huddy was taken from newspapers accounts of the trials, most particularly, the *Times* of London, the *Guardian* of London, the *Dublin Daily Express*, and the *Morning News*, Belfast, as well as records from the Parnell Commission and parliamentary reports on "Parnellism and Crime." In many of the newspaper articles, the given names are omitted and, occasionally, vary from one report to the next (such as the Burkes implicated in the Mountmorres murder). Reported distances also varied depending on the estimates of those testifying at the various trials. In some cases, witnesses were asked to clarify whether they were referencing an Irish mile (2,240 yards) or an English mile (1,760 yards).

I used numerous sources for the purpose of gaining an understanding of what Ireland was like during the Land War, including, but not limited to, Kerby Miller's exhaustive account of Irish emigration, *Emigrants and Exiles*, Father Jarlath Waldron's definitive *The Maamtrasna Murders*, Professor Pat Finnegan's *Loughrea, 'That Den of Infamy,' The Land War in Co. Galway, 1879-82*, and R. F. Foster's *Modern Ireland 1600-1972*. The conclusions are mine and subject to change based on new information. I consider this book to be an ongoing project. If anyone has any information that can add to or clarify what I have written, I may be contacted at quailcreekpub@hotmail.com.

Additional information supplementing many of the chapters can be found in the "Notes" section. Sources for quotes are listed in the "Sources" section at the end of the book.

Timeline - 1868-1949

1868   William Gladstone becomes Prime Minister at the head of a Liberal majority government.

1869   The Church of Ireland is disestablished.

1870   The Land Act of 1870 (Ireland) is largely ineffectual in addressing tenant issues.

1871   The Protection of Life and Property (Ireland) Act 1871 (aka The Coercion Act—one of several) permits the arrest and detention without trial of persons reasonably suspected of membership in a secret society.

1875   Charles Stewart Parnell is elected as Member of Parliament for County Meath.

1878   April - William Sydney Clements, 3rd Lord Leitrim, is assassinated near Milford, Donegal.

1878-80   Mini-famine in the West of Ireland

1879   Irish National Land League is founded for the purpose of campaigning for the three "Fs": fixity of tenure, fair rents, and free sale. The first monster meeting is held in Irishtown, Mayo and attended by thousands.

1880-81   The Bessborough Commision, under the chairmanship of the 6th Earl of Bessborough, concludes that the 1870 Land Act affords tenants no real protection. Four of the five commissioners declare in favor of the three "Fs."

1880   September - The "boycott" is employed in County Mayo against Captain Charles Boycott. Three weeks after its implementation, Lord Mountmorres is assassinated near his home, Ebor Hall, in Dooroy, Galway.

1881   A set of campaigns against high rents begins and develops into a crusade against the power of landlords (the "Land Wars").

1881	January - The Protection of Life and Property (Ireland) Act 1881 (aka The Coercion Act) permits the arrest and detention without trial of persons reasonably suspected of membership in a secret society.
1881	The Land Law (Ireland) Act of 1881 establishes the principle of dual ownership by landlord and tenant, gives legal status to the Ulster Custom of the three "Fs" throughout the country, provides for compensation for improvements, and creates the Irish Land Commission and a land court.
1881	The "No Rent Manifesto" is issued by Charles Stewart Parnell from his cell in Kilmainham Jail, Dublin. The manifesto calls for a campaign of passive resistance by the entire population of tenant farmers by withholding rents for the purpose of obtaining rent abatements under the Land Act of 1881.
1882	January - Joseph and John Huddy, bailiff of Lord Ardilaun and his grandson, are murdered in Upper Cloughbrack, Galway.
1882	May - Frederick Cavendish, Chief Secretary of Ireland, and William Burke, Permanent Under-secretary, are assassinated in Phoenix Park, Dublin.
1882	August - Maamtrasna Massacre - Five members of the John Joyce family are murdered in the mountains of Maamtrasna, County Galway (now a part of County Mayo).
1882	The Crimes Act is passed giving the Government in Dublin greater summary powers.
1882	The 1882 Amending Act, also known as the Arrears Act, is negotiated between Parnell and Gladstone while Parnell is incarcerated in Kilmainham Jail. The act empowers the Land Commission to cancel arrears of less than thirty pounds owed by tenants. An estimated two million pounds in arrears is taken off the books.
1886	First Home Rule Bill is defeated in the House of Commons.
1887	Amendment to the 1882 Amending Act extends the terms of that act to include leaseholders.

1890	Charles Stewart Parnell is involved in a divorce scandal with Mrs. Katherine O'Shea, dividing the Irish Party.
1891	Charles Stewart Parnell dies.
1893	In London, the Second Home Rule Bill is defeated in the House of Lords.
1914	The Third Home Rule Bill is passed and immediately suspended due to the belief that Britain will soon be at war with Germany and the Austrian-Hungarian Empire.
1916-49	The Easter Rising in Dublin is followed by a war for independence, a civil war, the Irish Free State, and, in 1949, the establishment of the Republic of Ireland.

Introduction

It is fair to say that Ireland has a tortured past. Its proximity to England proved irresistible to the English. After Henry II claimed Ireland as his own in 1171, English monarchs doled out large swaths of land to a chosen few. In succeeding centuries, battles raged between the Irish and their better-armed enemies, until, in 1690, Catholic James II was thoroughly trounced by his Protestant son-in-law and throne usurper, William III of Orange, at the Battle of the River Boyne, just north of Dublin.

Even though William III did an admirable job in beating James II and his Irish supporters, no one could wreak havoc quite like Oliver Cromwell, a Puritan zealot, who rode with God whispering in his ear. After Charles I's execution in 1649, many Royalists fled to Ireland hoping to keep their heads on their shoulders rather than at the bottom of a basket. Unfortunately, Cromwell had a long reach, and his men pursued them and their Irish hosts with a vengeance. The West of Ireland is littered with the ruins of abbeys and churches torched by Cromwell's men.

In 1652, the Act of Settlement was passed by the Rump Parliament of Cromwell's Commonwealth. This act rewarded creditors who had financed Cromwell's wars, as well as Protestant Ulstermen, with land confiscated from soldiers, clergy, and anyone else who got in their way. But what was one to do with all those pesky people who remained on the land? The answer: Welcome to Connaught.

Included in Cromwell's "relocations" were my relations, some of whom were pushed so far west that they ended up living on Omey, a tidal island off the Galway coast that was described by a nineteenth-century traveler as a "spewy marsh" that "rivals for barrenness and wretchedness any other spot in all of Connemara."

But why Connaught? I shall allow a geologist to explain: "Heath, bog, and rock prevail everywhere; much of the ground is mountainous, with numerous lofty summits looking down on lake strewn barren lowlands." Or as one botanist put it: "Taken as a whole, the province of Connaught is not an ideal agricultural district."

The result of this forced migration of Irish Catholics was that in 1876, "less than 800 landlords owned half the country; 302 owned 33.7% of Irish land; and 15,527 (80.5 percent) owned 19.3 percent."

The Land Act of 1870 attempted to remedy this imbalance but proved inadequate, and a mini-famine in 1877-1879 exacerbated a growing discontent among the Irish peasantry as manifested in the emergence of the Home Rule and tenant-rights movements. An outlet for so much frustration appeared in the fall of 1879 when James Daly and Michael Davitt of County Mayo proposed the formation of the Land League, an organization whose purpose was the return of Irish soil to the Irish and an end to "landlordism." But in the three years of the League's existence, violence descended on Ireland, and Joyce Country, a part of County Galway, became known as "A Murderer's Country."[1]

The *Guardian* of London, no friend of the Land League, described this part of Galway as a "nest of assassins, the breeding ground of assassination. Since the beginning of these troubles, undetected murder after undetected murder, has been committed in that region, culminating in the ghastly deed which we report today," that is, the massacre of the Joyce family in the mountains of Maamtrasna, now a part of County Mayo.

In September 1884, the *Times* of London featured a series of articles from various parts of the Emerald Isle. In "Letters from the West of Ireland," the *Times* correspondent provided a tour of Connaught, and it serves as a primer on conditions existing in Galway at a time of widespread agrarian unrest, that unrest leading to the assassination of Lord Mountmorres, as well as the murders of Joseph and John Huddy, bailiff of Lord Ardilaun and his grandson:

---

[1] Joyce Country encompasses the land between Lough Mask and Lough Corrib. Moving counterclockwise are the villages of Maam, Cornamona, Cong, The Neale, Clonbur, Tourmakeady, Cloghbrack, Finney, and Leenane. The original Joyce was Thomas Joyce, who immigrated to the area from Wales at the beginning of the fourteenth century. See map on page 51.

"A few miles further, we came upon the little Mountmorres property, but prettily planted, an enclave in the great estates of Lord Ardilaun. It was the property of the unfortunate Lord Mountmorres, and inquiring who occupied the house at present, I was told that it is also tenanted by policemen. In fact, no small number of men must be indispensable to picket and patrol even the more uninhabitable outskirts of that savage and inaccessible country... Here the aborigines have scarcely been disturbed from time immemorial. Nine-tenths of them are said to bear the names of the ancient septs of the Joyces or the Coynes.

"Lord Mountmorres's house was made familiar to English people by the many views of it in the illustrated papers at the time of the murder... It looks more like the residence of a second-rate Mid-Lothian [Scotland] farmer than of a nobleman... My friendly driver... pulled up before a gap in a loose stone wall, which had evidently been repaired comparatively recently. Either by change or designedly, the top stone in the breach was a small black slab, much like a tombstone in miniature; and that slab marks the spot where the ruffians fired on their victim.

"And to have done with the melancholy list of outrages, the next day, Mr. Burke, Lord Ardilaun's agent, pointed from the high grounds in Ashford-park to a strangely beautiful scene among the lovely Lough Mask mountains... 'That,' said Mr. Burke, 'is the point of Kilbride; up the valley among those high hills to the left is Maamtrasna [site of the massacre of the John Joyce family]; while the lough arm winding at the back of the promontory is Cloughbrack, where the Huddies—the bailiffs who were sewn up in sacks—were thrown into the water by their murderers.'

"All that country through which we have been passing since we left Leenane is unfit for human habitation; and we may read the consequences of its misappropriation in its record of outrages and crimes. Great parts of it belong to Arthur Guinness, Lord Ardilaun, notoriously one of the most liberal landlords in Ireland; but when his lordship's father bought it, he had to take over the starving paupers with the land, and he could not get rid of them if he would. Thanks to emigration, they are thinning now, and a happy thing it is for all parties. Yet this wild valley is rich in the extreme, were it only turned to its natural uses... With some judicious hill-draining, we should say in

Scotland that it has magnificent ground for a first-class deer forest. How far the deer would do well on these bare Connaught hills, in the West Irish damp, I do not know, and in any case, the surrounding peasants would soon make short work of them."

Without any real awareness, the *Times* correspondent described the yawning gap between landlord and tenant in County Galway. While Lord Ardilaun could appreciate the wild beauty of the two lakes and surrounding countryside, his tenants dealt with the cruel reality of farming and grazing on land consisting of depleted soils and inferior grasses. Today, a tour of this part of Galway shows that it remains fit only for the grazing of sheep, its acres dominated by gorse and cheat grass that the sheep give a wide berth in their search for edible grasses. But it *is* beautiful, with the landscape and colors changing in the Maamturks Mountains and the Twelve Pins with every passing cloud.[2]

But even in this barren soil, a seed had taken root—that of the right of an Irishman to own the acres he tilled. The first step in that direction began with a particularly savage murder of an Irish lord in the equally wild County Donegal.

---

[2] In his *Irish Sketchbook*, William Makepeace Thackery, author of *Vanity Fair*, described the Twelve Pins (also known as the Twelve Bens): "I won't attempt to pile up big words in place of those wild mountains over which the clouds as they passed, or the sunshine as it went and came, cast every variety of tint, light, and shadow. All one can do is to lay down the pen and ruminate, and cry 'Beautiful!' once more."

Chapter 1
Vigilante Justice in Donegal

In 1827, William Lamb, the future Lord Melbourne, Queen Victoria's Prime Minister, in an attempt to understand the unrest in Ireland, arranged to meet with some of the leaders of the "Irish agitation." According to Melbourne's friend, Sir Philip Champton, Melbourne was "involuntarily moved by the touching recitals of wrong and oppression which daily drove the peasantry to madness, and disdained to hide his disgust at the manner in which criminal justice was administered by exclusive juries and a partisan Bench... After listening to details of the vengeance wreaked on agents and underlings, he very characteristically exclaimed, 'Why don't they [the tenants] go at the big 'uns [the landlords].'" In 1878, they did.

A harbinger of the violence that arose out of the agrarian-reform movement, known as the Land War, was the assassination of William Sydney Clements, 3rd Earl of Leitrim, on April 2, 1878, near his Donegal estate. Although there were cries of outrage at his murder, few were actually sorry he was dead as he was despised by people of all creeds and class, but his death did result in considerable discomfort among the landowners. Were they next?

The Clements family came by their properties as a result of a grant of land from James I, Great Britain's first Stuart monarch, carved from the Plantation of Ulster. The first Lord Leitrim added extensively to his properties located in various parts of Ireland, including County Donegal and County Galway. The murder victim, William Sydney Clements, was born in Dublin in 1806. He chose the army as a profession, and in 1831, was promoted to captain and appointed to serve as an aide-de-camp to the Lord Lieutenant of Ireland. With the death of his elder brother in 1835, he became Viscount Clements, Member of Parliament for Country Leitrim, a county wedged between Counties Sligo and Donegal in Ireland's Northwest. Upon his father's death in 1854, Clements succeeded to the title just four years after the end of Ireland's greatest crisis, the Great Famine.

Leitrim was an unpleasant man on the best of days, and there were few of those. In an article recounting the life of the murdered lord, the *New York Times* wrote: "As he rose in riches, he fell in reputation, and there was not in the whole country a man more despised by those of his own rank, more loathed by those below it."

In 1863, Leitrim instructed the manager of a hotel he owned in Maam, Galway (the site now occupied by Keane's Bar, Maam Bridge) to refuse a room to the Earl of Carlisle, then serving as Lord Lieutenant of Ireland, in retaliation for an earlier slight. In preparation for the earl's visit, Carlisle's men went to the Maam hotel, at which time, the manager produced a letter written by Leitrim detailing His Lordship's instructions not to let a room to Carlisle under any circumstance. Alerted by his men to Leitrim's plot, the earl pushed on to a hotel in Cong (now Ryan's Hotel). But the insult to Her Majesty's representative in Ireland did not go unpunished. The earl was removed as a magistrate from the Commission of the Peace in Donegal, Leitrim, and Galway, and the Maam hotel lost its liquor license.

By the time William Sydney Clements became Earl of Leitrim, Ireland was no stranger to agrarian violence. Secret "ribbon or riband" societies, such as the Whiteboys, Captain Moonlight, and Captain Rory of the Hills, first appeared in the second decade of the nineteenth century. The name is derived from a green ribbon worn by members in their buttonholes as a badge

The purpose of these secret societies was to protect tenants by "persuading" a landlord that it was in his best interest not to pursue eviction. Methods might take the form of a threatening letter featuring a coffin, a rock thrown through a window, maimed livestock, bullets fired at his house, clipped ears, kneecapping, etc., and the occasional murder. These localized acts of intimidation resulted, in 1848, in the suspension of Habeas Corpus during the Great Famine as a result of a dramatic increase in crime, mostly against property, and again in 1866, in response to the rise of the Fenian Brotherhood, a group committed to the establishment of an independent Ireland. In some areas of the West, Fenianism "merged with existent Ribbon societies and adopted their ethos of the establishment of a republic by any means possible." The 1866 Suspension Act, aimed to suppress the Fenian movement, succeeded in driving many Fenians out of Ireland, many going to the United States, where they raised money for national causes.

If anyone made a case for the advancement of tenant rights in Ireland, it was Lord Leitrim. Before the 1870 Land Act, his tenants were without protection of any kind and subject to eviction with little notice. In order to keep his tenants in a perpetual state of unease, every eleven months, Leitrim's tenants were served with notices to quit before new leases were signed.

When approached by a tenant to appeal an eviction, Leitrim's favorite phrase was: "Go to hell or America." Shortly before his murder, he had signaled to his Galway tenants that it was his intention to "cast a rod on Lough Mask," and while he was fishing, his bailiffs would be "evicting twenty tenants in the Maam Valley."

In 1869, the *New York Tribune* wrote of the various covenants made by Irish tenants with Lord Leitrim. It illustrates how Leitrim's tenants were little better than feudal serfs:

> The lease is from year to year, determined by six months' notice... It reserves all timber, bogs, mines, game, hares, rabbits, wild fowl and fish, with the right of shooting, etc., to Lord Leitrim, his heirs and assigns...and gives him power to enter for the purpose of surveying, searching for minerals, and making roads and drains.
>
> The tenant is restrained from making new roads, fences, or drains on the land, and from building and altering any house thereon, and from allowing any house thereon to be used as a dwelling house, except that in which he himself resides, and he is also under stringent conditions as to tillage. He is to keep in repair, and to yield up in repair all buildings, etc. He is to dig up or cut down all thistles, docks, and other weeds, before they go to seed, or at any time when desired to do so by the said Earl of Leitrim. The tenant is also to assist to the utmost the said Earl in prosecuting trespassers.
>
> If he breaks any of these conditions, he is to be subject to a further rent, in the nature of liquidated damages.... Finally, nothing in the lease contained is to entitle the tenant to any payment of compensation for any farm or other building for agriculture or otherwise, or for any fixture or improvements of any description, unless the making of such work or

improvement shall have been previously stipulated for and specified by any agreement in writing.

It is easy to imagine the absolute despair Leitrim's tenants experienced under his tyrannical rule and the fear that must have gripped them when they saw His Lordship's carriage go by. Was it possible that a neglected thistle might end with their eviction?

As most of Leitrim's tenants were Catholics, they felt the pointed end of his policies. As a result, he was the target of assassination attempts and frequently received threats against his life, such as the one below from 1863:

> Lord Leitrim – Leave the County for we will not let you live to be doing harm to the poor. By the blessed Mary we will shoot you if you don't change your ways and act like a man, be off for revenge... I have thought it right to give you a notice that you might get time to repent you old lame beggar be off at once or you will get the contents of the gun that shot both Nixon, Murray, and Grierson. By God you shall, we will not let you go on ruining the poor. Go off to England and learn to be good, you have a new agent we hear [Mr. Wilson], so now is your time to change. Let the McAteers into their land at Doughbeg and take my advice, for if not you will be shot, and sent to hell the first time you are down here in Fannett [Fanad]. Let the Coolback men have sea weed and behave yourself. Obey these orders. If you don't want to get GOOD SHOT.

Lord Leitrim's response to the Lord Lieutenant was immediate:

> Milford, Strabane, May 19, 1863
>
> My Lord, I enclose to your Excellency a letter I have just received, and I have not the slightest doubt on my mind that it is the handwriting of Sub-Inspector Studdert of the Police. I have also to remark that the paper is very similar to that which has been recently used by him, and which is now before me.
>
> I am, my Lord, your obedient servant, LEITRIM

Leitrim wrote a second letter on May 20th to the Lord Lieutenant in which he encouraged the arrest of Studdert, and a third letter on June 9th in which he complained of the want of protection. As Leitrim was despised by his tenants, it was a reasonable worry. After careful examination, the County Inspector indicated that there was not the "remotest similarity" between the handwriting of the letter writer and Studdert, and the case was dismissed.

An article, "Lord Leitrim Again," published in December 1863 in the *London Review of Politics, Society, Literature, Art, & Science*, skewered the earl:

> In May last, Lord Leitrim—who is, as we have said, an unfortunate person—was unlucky enough to receive a threatening letter. Amongst his other misfortunes, Lord Leitrim at the time was at feud with an inspector of constabulary in his neighbourhood. In an evil hour his lordship put two and two together, and jumped at the conclusion that the inspector was the author of the malignant and anonymous epistle… The letter itself was of the usual infamous description. Among other very Irish-looking insults, characteristically enough it denounced his lordship as "a lame old beggar;" and…as Lord Leitrim's temper does not seem to bear trifling with or tampering with, that excellent nobleman must have felt very angry indeed on receiving it.
>
> Who the McAteers are, and why they are kept out of their land at Doughbeg, is a question between that estimable and oppressed family and his lordship; nor do we propose to discuss the respective rights of Lord Leitrim and "the Coolback" men to seaweed. These things are an allegory; they point to something beyond. They are part of a crop of controversies of which we get a glimpse in the background, and which are doubtless part of Lord Leitrim's misfortunes. It is his lordship's unhappy destiny to be at war both with the Government and his neighbours, and his tenantry and the police.

It was not just Catholics whom Leitrim targeted. In January 1858, he evicted a Presbyterian minister from his home even though Reverend White had "paid his rent regularly, gave the agent no trouble, and was, besides, an improving tenant." Unfortunately, the parson was guilty of relying on the Ulster custom of fixity of tenure, but custom is not law, and the ejectment proceeded. Another evictee was the constabulary at Milford with the result that when Mr. Wilson, Leitrim's agent, became a target of the Ribbon society and was shot, it took the constables two hours to arrive at the scene.

It is possible that as a Member of the House of Lords, Leitrim anticipated that with the passage of the Land Act of 1870, he would have to compensate his tenants for improvements made to the land and its building if they surrendered their lease. The law also made provision for damages for tenants evicted for causes other than non-payment of rent as well as compensation for disturbance—a polite way of saying that the tenant had been involuntarily removed from his farm. Most important for his Donegal estates in Ulster, the 1870 act established *in law* fixity of tenure, that is, a tenant could not be evicted if he met the obligations of his lease. Obviously, the provisions of the 1870 Land Act did nothing to improve His Lordship's temperament, and he was one of eight peers to protest against the legislation in the House of Lords.

The passage of the 1870 act incensed Leitrim, and his refusal to follow the law embroiled him in endless litigation with his tenants. His refusal to accept the rulings of the Land Courts resulted in several of the cases going from one tribunal to the next, some ending up being decided in the House of Lords where Leitrim sat. More often than not, the litigation served its intended purpose. Most of Leitrim's tenants, too poor to respond to endless legal challenges, waved the white flag and surrendered their farms.

But it was not heartless evictions alone that raised the ire of Leitrim's tenants. It was widely believed that Leitrim helped himself to the local lasses. American James Redpath, then on a tour of Ireland as a reporter for the *New York Tribune*, asked these questions: "Did Lord Leitrim not bear the reputation of being one of the vilest lepers in social life? Don't his tenants say that he flung a score at least of young girls into the brothels of Liverpool and New York…? Is it not believed by every one that he was killed on account of his personal offences…?"

Even the obituary printed in the *Londonderry Standard*, the leading Presbyterian organ of Derry, after mentioning the deceased's "virtues," revealed Leitrim's true character as someone who "punished with eviction every show of opposition to his will by his tenantry. If they cut seaweed, eviction;[3] if they objected to his capriciously taking away a

---

[3] Any seaweed that washed ashore was the property of the landholder closest to that segment of shoreline. (In law, the owner had "the rights of land and sea."). Any

piece of land to give to someone else, eviction; *if they refused the pick of the family for domestic service of his lordship,* eviction!" The last charge was a euphemism for demanding that the prettiest girls be taken into His Lordship's *personal* service, and it may be the reason why, when he was assassinated, he was repeatedly shot, clubbed with the butt of a gun until the gunstock split in half, and turned upside down in a pool of water to drown.

The three assassins, Nial Shiels of Doaghmore, an itinerant tailor, Michael Heraghty of Tullyconnell, and Michael McElwee of Ballyworiskey, were from the remote Fanad Peninsula of the far north of Donegal.[4] Fiona Slevin's blog, *Lough Rynn*, describes the murderers' route to Cratlagh Wood in their dogged pursuit of Leitrim:

> On the night before that arranged for the shooting, April 1st, Michael McElwee came to the home of Nial Shiels in Doaghmore at 10 o'clock to make arrangements for the following day. Both left Doaghmore at 11:30 and picked up Heraghty on their way. The three were armed with the muzzle-loading guns of the time, charged with heavy slugs. They proceeded to Muineagh [twelve miles from Doaghmore], and from the seashore took a boat and crossed to the Rossguill side [western side of Mulroy Bay] where they changed boats. They again put to sea and arrived at Cratlagh Wood about 7 a.m. where they took up positions on the shore side of the road to await the arrival of Leitrim. While waiting a pedestrian passed. Suspecting that he…would give information to the authorities in Milford, it was decided that Heraghty "shadow" him. Heraghty left, leaving his gun behind.

Early on the morning of April 2, 1878, Lord Leitrim set out on the three-mile journey from Manor Vaughan, an estate described as a

---

harvest of seaweed without permission was regarded as theft. Seaweed is a rich source of vitamins and minerals and has high levels of protein and iron and may be the reason why many families living on coastal farms survived the Famine. It was also used as fertilizer in potato and turnip patches.

[4] The previous year, McElwee's father became involved in litigation with Lord Leitrim with the result that McElwee was rendered bankrupt, and his house and farm were sold at auction in June 1877. For more information on McElwee, see Chapter 1, Notes.

"dilapidated bachelor mansion" on the shore of Mulroy Bay, for Milford, a village he owned in its entirety. Usually, a patrol of armed police would have met His Lordship halfway, but on the day of his murder, Leitrim started half an hour earlier. Always in fear of being waylaid, he carried two guns on his person.[5] The site of the ambush was a dip in the road near Cratlagh Wood.

There were two cars in the party. The first was the Milford Hotel coach carrying Lord Leitrim, the Court Clerk John Makim, and a young coachman, Charles Buchanan.[6] The second car held Lord Leitrim's coachman and valet, William Kincaid, and Michael Logue the owner and driver of the car. This car was slowed down with a heavy load of the Earl's luggage and by having a lame horse...

The first Kincaid knew of the incident was a report from a volley of several shots below him on the road. Looking towards the sound, he saw jets of smoke from the guns. Charles Buchanan had been shot in the head and died immediately... John Makim the clerk, was also shot in the head but managed to stumble back towards the second car. He died later.

Lord Leitrim never got a chance to get to either of the guns he carried. One of the first shots hit him in the right arm, fracturing his elbow joint and he took nine or ten bullets... He fell to the ground and the horses galloped away. Two of the assassins, Michael McElwee and Neil Shiels, went to finish him but he managed to get to his feet and struggled fiercely with the two. Even at 72 and suffering gunshot wounds, Lord Leitrim was strong enough to wrestle with his attackers. When he was found later, he was still clutching a portion of a red beard with

---

[5] In his 1902 *On an Irish Jaunting-Car*, Samuel G. Bayne, Irish immigrant and New York banker, stated that "as a boy I have been more than once startled by the appearance of a pair of cars with eight men on them, each having a couple of double-barreled shotguns. Lord Leitrim was one of them; the others were his guards, going to Milford to collect the rents." Leitrim was entitled to police protection under the Peace Preservation Act of 1870 and was one of the first to apply for assistance.

[6] According to the *Times* of London, "The car appeared to have been driven by a man [Charles Buchanan] who came from Derry on the previous Sunday and who sat in the coachman's seat of the cart." (July 20, 1878)

which he had dragged his assassin around the road until Shiels finally struck him down with the butt of a gun.

It was reported that after the murders, the killers got in a boat and calmly rowed across Mulroy Bay, returning to their homes on the Fanad Peninsula. According to one British source, "On the evening of the day on which the murder took place, Milford was illuminated and a general carouse was held."

The undiluted hatred Lord Leitrim provoked was demonstrated at his funeral at St. Michan's Church, Dublin: "The mob wanted to wreak their drunken rage on the dead body of the old Earl, as if it was not enough that he had been murdered; and when they were disappointed in their charitable desire to throw the corpse into the street, they howled and yelled an accompaniment of brutal hate to the funeral service. It was a disgraceful affair, scarcely possible in any other latitude of the civilized world." In fear for their lives, family members remained at the church. Only his heir accompanied the coffin to the family vault.

The writer, a correspondent for the *New York Times*, obviously lacked an understanding of Irish rituals. It was not unusual for the Irish to interact with a corpse before he was sent on his way, usually with a drink in hand. In Leitrim's case, he got the send-off he deserved.

The earl's presumed heir, Robert Bermingham Clements, offered an award of £10,000 for the apprehension and conviction of the killers. A group of magistrates established a fund for the arrest of the murderers that raised £6,000, and the Government offered a paltry £500. (They didn't like him, either.) Despite the lure of reward money, no snitch came forward. Eventually, three men were charged with his death, none of whom actually committed the murder. A fund, raised locally and from supporters in the United States, particularly Philadelphia, was provided for the men's legal defense.

Unlike most murders committed in Ireland, this one did not end with Irish Catholics being hung from a gibbet behind the walls of a county jail. "Eleven men were arrested for the crime but eight were soon discharged. The three men who remained in custody were brothers Bernard and Thomas McGranahan and Michael Heraghty. The gun butt had been traced to Heraghty, and paper for the wadding used to load the rifle was traced to a school copybook owned by the McGranahans. Heraghty, who had been arrested in April, died in

Lifford Jail in October of typhus while awaiting trial. The McGranahans were released from Lifford Jail for a lack of evidence in February 1879.[7] At the Londonderry train station, their release was met with jubilation: "The Coal Porters' Band, followed by a dense crowd of youths of the lower order, marched, with the two peasants in their midst, to the railway station."

The actual murderers were never arrested. McElwee died of a fever shortly after the murders, but before being implicated, and Shiels lived until 1921. In 1960, a Celtic cross monument was erected in Fanad, not in memory of Lord Leitrim, but for the "patriots" who had killed him.

Although Leitrim's murder was welcomed by the vast majority of his tenants, there *was* collateral damage. In anticipation of additional violence following Leitrim's murder, the Government imposed a tax for the maintenance of additional police barracks. This was an added burden on an already poor tenantry. In one case, a police constable, who had been tasked with collecting the tax, found that he could "find nothing to seize. So great was the defaulter's poverty that the collector went to the nearest provision shop and bought food for the family, who were starving." Fortunately, the Government reconsidered, and the tax was removed. With Leitrim's death, the district was, at long last, in a peaceful state.[8]

Leitrim's murder was an indicator that, under the surface, the Irish tenantry was seething at the hopelessness of their situation. Although Leitrim was their most notable victim, he would not be their last.

---

[7] The Lifford jail is forty-two miles from Doaghmore, along narrow roads and difficult terrain, making visits from families of the accused next to impossible.

[8] A similar tax was imposed on the people of Joyce Country during the Land War as it was necessary to have police huts, housing eight constables each, throughout the district.

Chapter 2
Years Leading up to the Formation of the Land League in 1879

The heartlessness of the 3rd Earl of Leitrim was an extreme example of landlordism. On the other hand, his actions provide an excellent example of the inherent powers vested in a landlord and the resulting agrarian crime that followed such heavy-handedness. Before the Land Act of 1870, evictions in Ireland, especially in the West, were as regular as Sunday mass. The table below shows the correlation between evictions and agrarian crime between 1849 and 1853, the last two years of the Great Famine and three subsequent years:

Year	Families Evicted	Agrarian Crime
1849	16,686	957
1850	19,949	1,362
1851	13,147	1,013
1852	8,591	913
1853	4838	469

Report of Special Commission 1888, Presented to Both Houses of Parliament on Command of Her Majesty - Evictions and Crime, 1849-1886

The decline in evictions in the years following the Great Famine resulted in a corresponding decrease in agrarian crime. Although evictions continued through the 1850s and 1860s, there was only a modest increase in agrarian crime. A possible explanation is that many Irish tenants were better off as a result of increased emigration from the congested districts, a pattern that continued well into the next century. Their relations, now living abroad in the United States,

Canada, and Australia, sent funds to their families in Ireland facilitated by a postal money-order agreement between the United Kingdom and the United States in 1871. This arrangement enabled the Irish to pay their rent, repair their cottages, and make improvements to their farms. It was also a source of passage money for additional emigration, thus reducing Ireland's surplus population.

Despite a reduction in crime, Britain realized it had an Irish problem. One attempt at amelioration was the Irish Church Act of 1869. That act replaced the 1823 Composition for Tithes Act that had required all citizens of Ireland, regardless of faith, to pay monetary tithes, instead of a percentage of crop yields, to support the Anglican Church of Ireland. This act was bitterly resented by Catholics and Ulster Presbyterians alike. The 1869 Irish Church Act, which took effect in January 1871, disestablished the Anglican Church in Ireland. That was a good first step.

In 1868, liberal politician William Ewart Gladstone became prime minister. During his election, he had campaigned on a platform of justice for Ireland that included land reform. The result was the passage of the Landlord and Tenant Act of 1870. The act accomplished three things:

(1) It established in law that no tenant could be evicted from his farm if he had paid his rent in full and on time.

(2) At the end of the lease, the landlord had to pay the tenant, if he had not been evicted, for any improvements made on the farm, such as installing drains, road repairs, and improvements to the cottage.

(3) The "John Bright" clause allowed tenants to borrow from the Government two-thirds of the cost of purchasing their holdings at five percent interest payable over thirty-five years *if* the landlord was *willing* to sell. However, few tenants were in a position to take advantage of these terms.[9]

---

[9] John Bright, Member of Parliament for Birmingham, in December, 1882, addressed the issue of agrarian unrest before Parliament: "When the law refuses its duty, when Government denies the right of a people, when competition is so fierce for the little land which the monopolists grant to cultivation in Ireland, when in fact for a bare potato millions are scrambling, these people are driven back from law and the usages

Most historians regard the 1870 act as a failure in that it fell short in clearly defining the rights of tenant and landlord. A major flaw was that the law applied only to yearly leases. Landlords got around that stipulation by issuing eleven-month leases, requiring annual renegotiation. Additionally, provisions covering compensation for improvements were limited by the complicated procedures necessary in claiming and assessing compensation. However, its greatest failure was that the Government would not control Irish rents as a capitalistic government must not interfere in private-property transactions.

The Bessborough Commission, a commission established to inquire into the workings of the 1870 act, reported that the act gave the tenant little protection because compensation for improvements could be claimed only if the tenant *gave up the lease*. It also forced tenants to accept rent increases often based on those same improvements. The Commission recommended the adoption of the "Three Fs," that is, fair rent, free sale, and fixity of tenure, as practiced for hundreds of years in the Province of Ulster.

With the passage of the 1870 Landlord and Tenant Act, progress had been made, but—as was always the case with Ireland—its implementation was slow and incremental, and there were many who were no longer willing to wait for change. It was their intention to rouse the Irish from their slumber and claim the land as their own.

---

of civilization to that which is termed the law of nature… And in this case, the people of Ireland believe…that it is only by these acts of vengeance periodically committed that they can hold in suspense the arm of the proprietor and the agent, who, in too many cases, if he dared, would exterminate them. At this moment…there is a war between landlord and tenant—a war as fierce, as relentless, as though it were carried on by force of arms."

Chapter 3
Mini-Famine: 1877-79
A Turning Point

God grant that mischief does not follow.
Patrick Duggan, Bishop of Clonfert

When compared to the grim half decade of the Great Famine (1845-1850), the first half of the 1870s were times of plenty for the Irish as prices for crops and livestock were good. But under the surface, there was widespread discontent with Ireland's British overlords who ruled every facet of the Irish-Catholic existence. In 1874, former British Prime Minister Benjamin Disraeli understood that Ireland was a pot that was very likely to come to a boil: "Neither liberty of the press nor liberty of the person exists in Ireland. Arrests are at all times liable. It is a fact that at any time in Ireland the police may enter into your house, examine your papers to see if there is any resemblance between the writing and that of some anonymous letter that has been sent to a third person. In Ireland, if a man writes an article in a newspaper and it offends, his paper may be suppressed. They say Ireland is peaceful. Yes, but is she so, not because she is contented, but because she is held under by coercive laws?" The answer to Disraeli's question is obvious.

Another disquieting element came into play with the harvest of 1877, a very wet year, particularly in the potato-dependent West. In that year, the potato yield was two tons per acre, a decrease from the decennial average of 3.2 tons per acre. In 1878, another wet year, the average was three tons, but then disaster hit in 1879 when the potato crop yield per acre was only 1.3 tons, "the poorest return ever obtained from the potato crop in Ireland during the whole period for which agricultural statistics have been collected."

In 1879, the worst year of the mini-famine, thousands went

begging for seed potatoes to replace the rotting tubers caused by too much rain as well as the seed potatoes they had eaten in their hunger. The Annual Register for 1879 reported: "As the season advanced, the distress became more apparent; the rain was continuous, and Ireland was threatened with a double calamity: a potato famine and a peat famine; for the potato crop was a failure, and as there was no sun to dry the peat, a fuel famine was imminent. Pauperism had increased…and bankruptcy amongst the farmers had grown more frequent."

The distress experienced by the Irish came to the attention of James Hack Tuke, an English Quaker, who had toured Ireland during the Great Famine and collaborated with Society of Friends relief workers to alleviate the effects of the crisis. Fearing another historic famine, Tuke set out for Ireland in February of 1880 for a six-week tour of Donegal and Connaught. His findings were recorded in a memoir of his life by his friend, Sir Edward Fry. He portrayed a country desperately in need of immediate intervention, and it merits quoting at length:

"The townland of Meenacladdy, Donegal stretches over a wide extent of wet bog-land… A turf dwelling, near the road, which my friends, who were not acquainted with the West, could not believe was a human habitation. The end of the house towards the road was not more than four or five feet high, but, as the ground sank rapidly on the other side, you were able to find an entrance through a low doorway. Within, at first, all appeared dark, the peat smoke which filled the room blinding us. When a little accustomed to the smoke, we saw, by the light which strayed in through the opening in the roof where the smoke ought to have gone out, but did not, a woman and several children crouched around a small fire. There was neither chair nor table in the place; probably one small stool was all they possessed in this way. The bedstead was covered with a little ragged coverlid, beneath which some straw was spread on the wooden frame; the children, or others who could not find room upon it, lay down on the bare rock or earth of the floor, in the thin clothes they wear all day, with a little straw or hay beneath them… Had it not been for the 'meal' [imported cornmeal], they must have starved. The man who seemed an industrious fellow, was working on the bog, in spite of the weather, seeking to cultivate a little ground for the coming season. He had neither cow nor sheep, only three or four fowls. He had been to Scotland for the harvest last autumn, but had come back without earnings, and now, in debt for meal and rent, he was beaten.

"Here is a picture of a visit on the Connemara coast: I will venture to say no one would think it possible that any human being could live or even find foothold on this rock-strewn shore; but, by degrees, you see the little 'smokes' arising, and here and there little dark strips of land, which show that the ground is being prepared for the potatoes they hope to obtain, for they have none left to plant. Then you see peering above the rocks little dark heads of men, women, and children, who, attracted by the unusual sight, come out of their cabins to reconnoitre. As you walk among them, they watch you with curious eyes; they do not beg, and cannot answer your enquiries, for…few can talk English. They are a race of wild people, poorly clad, and living with the cattle in their houses, often lying on the damp ground on hay like them. No distribution of meal had taken place last week, and several families were sitting round small quantities of the smallest (old) potatoes I ever saw, and with nothing else to eat with them…"

Although the following was intended as a humorous break in the unrelieved misery of the people encountered by the relief workers, it must be noted that this event took place in a country that was a part of the greatest empire the world had seen since the fall of Rome.

"Mr. H. A. Robinson, a local Government Inspector, wrote to Tuke as follows: "The number of letters I receive from people asking for seed [potatoes] averages about 600 a day. I have forbidden all notes being sent, but it is no use; the people have the most firm belief that 'a writin' is infallible; and, as I will not receive them, they resort to strategy and skillful subterfuge, and pop the 'writins' through the windows, under the doors, and into every available nook and cranny… This morning, when I took in my boots from outside the hotel door, the toes were crammed with these mysterious missives… The 'writins' themselves are extraordinary specimens, and any of the people that are unable to write repair to a certain scribe, the efficacy of whose effusions is acknowledged…

"I never saw any people so overwhelming in their protestations of gratitude as they are to them that's sending the potatoes. If ever you come to Erris [Mayo] again, you will meet with a warm reception. Rivers will be netted for you, mountains will be poached in your honor, poteen will be publicly made for your especial delectation, and God help the unlucky landlord, policeman, or ganger that will dare to interfere with the grateful acknowledgment of a thankful peasantry, to the grandest gintleman that iver kem amongst them."

In 1879, the potato crop was not the only crop affected. Yields of wheat, oats, barley, and turnips were also below average. Due to flooded fields, the hay crop could not be harvested. The lack of potatoes also resulted in a reduction in the number of pigs and poultry. As a result of an increasingly poor diet, there was a rise in diseases, such as typhus and pellagra.

Unlike the Great Famine of 1845-1850, the Irish mini-famine of 1877-1879 caused widespread hunger, especially in the West, rather than mass starvation. The decrease in mortality from previous famines was due, most significantly, to a prompt response by the British Government and the presence of a railway system that allowed for the distribution of food in a matter of days rather than weeks as was the case in the Great Famine. Another factor in preventing starvation was aid from a world-wide community of Irish expatriates, especially those who had immigrated to the United States. Irishmen living abroad responded to numerous newspaper appeals like those of the *New York Tribune*. The *Tribune's* owner, James Gordon Bennet, donated $100,000 of his own money for Irish relief. Additionally, the Land League donated £60,000 from funds raised in America.

In an effort to reach remote communities, the British Government deployed gunboats, loaded with supplies, to coastal communities in the West, and in March 1880, the U.S. Department of the Navy sent the *USS Constellation* to Ireland with a cargo of clothing and over 3,300 barrels of food. And more was on its way.

Despite intervention from abroad, the tenants remained in dire straits. With so many in distress, assistance was spread thin. With no crops to sell, it was impossible to pay the rent as it is estimated that for most tenants in the West, forty percent of their income was spent on rent. Matters were exacerbated by falling prices caused by the importation of cheap grain from America as well as imports of meat from as far away as Australia and Argentina.

At the time of the mini-famine, many Irish were alive who had survived the Great Famine, and lessons had been learned. "The Irish peasants concluded that a potato crop failure was likely to lead to famine, that a famine would probably cause a destructive pestilence [disease], and that many of the landlords, perhaps the majority of them, would take advantage of famine and pestilence to push their rights to the limit, thus depriving thousands of sick and starving people of a home."

The question was: Would Irish landlords recognize their duties to their tenants as well as their rights as landlords? The answer can be found in the rise in evictions during the years of the mini-famine and the concurrent rise of the Land League. Declining figures for evictions and agrarian crime in 1882 and 1883 demonstrate the effects depopulation in the congested districts, as a result of emigration, had on crime:[10]

Year	Families Evicted	Agrarian Crime
1877	463	236
1878	980	301
1879	1,238	863
1880	2,110	2,590
1881	3,415	4,489
1882	5,201	3,432
1883	3,643	870

Report of Special Commission 1888, Presented to Both Houses of Parliament on Command of Her Majesty - Evictions and Crime, 1849-1886

The failed harvests of 1877 and 1878, and the particularly bleak harvest of 1879, proved to be fertile soil for the Land League, a movement whose purpose was to wrest the land from the landlords and return it to the Irish. Although the men who created the Land League condemned violence, there was a tacit understanding that their audience was hearing a different message. After decades of frustration in dealing with the status quo, some sought redress of their grievances with a gun.

---

[10] Statistics for 1879 show that 47,364 people, an increase of 5,738 over the previous year, left Ireland. In 1880, emigration numbers nearly doubled when 95,857 persons left Ireland ("Emigration Statistics of Ireland"). In Galway, in 1841, the population was 440,000. In 1881, it was 242,000. It would reach a low of 149,000 in 1971.

Chapter 4
The Land League

It is the old battle with new banners and new war-cries but waged against the same old foe.
American Land League Supporter James Redpath

Prior to 1879, violent responses to agrarian issues had been localized. All that changed with the emergence of two men who would lead the land-reform movement: Michael Davitt, an Irish-Catholic who had been born into extreme poverty in County Mayo,[11] and Charles Stewart Parnell, an affluent Protestant landlord from County Wicklow and a member of Parliament. Davitt, who had been imprisoned in England for Fenian activities, took the first step in rousing the masses to an ancient claim: Ireland for the Irish. Devoting himself to the cause of avoiding famine and eviction, Michael Davitt organized a meeting of tenants in County Mayo and was able to secure a twenty-five percent reduction in rent in his home county. This success set in motion a campaign for a national reduction of rents, an end to evictions, and the long-term goal of transferring ownership of land from landlord to tenant. Toward this end, Davitt persuaded Charles Stewart Parnell to make a speech at a meeting of tenant farmers in Westport, County Mayo, in the summer of 1879:

> A fair rent is a rent the tenant can reasonably afford to pay according to the times, but in bad times a tenant cannot be expected to pay as much as he did in good times. Now what must we do in order to induce the landlords to see that position? You must show them that you intend to hold a firm grip of your

---

[11] Davitt's family was evicted from their farm in Straide, County Mayo when Michael was six. While the family watched, the roof was set on fire and the house leveled. The site of the farm is visible from the cemetery in Straide Abbey where Davitt is buried.

homesteads and lands. You must not allow yourselves to be dispossessed as your fathers were dispossessed in 1847… You must help yourselves, and the public opinion of the world will stand by you, and support you in your struggle to defend your homestead.

After three years of poor crop yields, current rents were no longer fair and must be adjusted to meet the reality of the situation on the ground. Additionally, for the first time, in front of a large crowd, the concept of peasant proprietorship was enunciated.

Land League activities were funded with American money, much of it collected at political meetings and Fenian picnics or in local bars. A significant portion of the funds was funneled through Patrick Ford's radical magazine, *Irish World*. "In 1879-1882, Irish Americans publicly remitted over $5 million to relieve Irish distress, sustain evicted tenants and finance the Land War." The highest percentage of donations from Americans to Land War activities came from among working-class immigrants in industrial neighborhoods, such as the hard and soft coalfields of Pennsylvania.

Some Land Leaguers suggested that fair rent rates should be based on the valuations given in Griffith's Valuation, a survey conducted between 1857-1864 by Richard Griffith, who had been appointed by Parliament for the purpose of establishing the value of every property in every county in Ireland. Although the idea was hugely popular among tenants, "the valuation was calculated at a time when prices were abnormally low, and had never been intended as a rental guide."[12]

The valuation was used for the purpose of establishing who would pay the poor rates that supported the local workhouse and outdoor relief. Once a family was evicted, they had to rely on the kindness of their relations, live out in the open, or enter a workhouse. Most people who lived in a workhouse were required to work on outdoor relief, such as repairing and building roads and bridges. According to the Poor Law Relief Act of 1843, as amended, if the value of the tenant's property was less than four pounds per annum, the burden of paying the poor rate fell to the lessor. Obviously, if there were fewer pauper

---

[12] After all was said and done, the Land Act of 1881 reduced rents approximately twenty percent, which came very close to the level of Griffith's valuation.

tenants living on the land, the landlord would have to pay less to the poor-law board, thus providing an incentive to evict or to encourage emigration.

The Griffith's Valuation survey for County Galway was completed on June 19, 1857. In that survey, for Glenlusk, a townland southwest of Clonbur in Joyce Country on the shores of Lough Corrib, lived John Lydon, my great-great-grandfather. Together with seven other tenants, Lydon farmed a 401-acre property, consisting of four islands "of no agricultural value," whose primary lessor was the infamous Earl of Leitrim. (The property was later purchased by Benjamin Guinness.) Of the names listed, not one person qualified to pay the poor law rate because the earnings of all eight tenants were four pounds or less.

No. and Letters of Reference to Map.	Names.		Description of Tenement.	Area.	Rateable Annual Valuation.		Total Annual Valuation of Rateable Property.
	Townlands and Occupiers.	Immediate Lessors.			Land.	Buildings.	
	Four small Islands in Lough Corrib, belonging to no agricultural value), ...	Benjamin L. Guinness (of	. . . .	0 1 10	—	—	—
1	GLENLUSK. (Ord. S. 39.) a Thomas Coyne, b Stephen Coyne, c John Hilleran, d Patrick Lyden, e Denis Lyden, f John Lyden, g John Toorusk, — Martin Lyden,	Earls of Leitrim and Charlemont, .	House and land, House and land, House and land, House, office, &land, House, office, & land, House, office, & land, House, office, & land, Land, . .	401 0 17	2 0 0 1 0 0 1 0 0 4 0 0 2 0 0 2 0 0 3 0 0 1 0 0	0 8 0 0 4 0 0 4 0 0 12 0 0 8 0 0 8 0 0 10 0 —	2 8 0 1 4 0 1 4 0 4 12 0 2 8 0 2 8 0 3 10 0 1 0 0
			Total, .	401 0 17	16 0 0	2 14 0	18 14 0
	Eight small Islands in Lough Corrib, belonging to agricultural value), .	Tenants of Glenlusk (of no	. . . .	6 0 21	—	—	—

The above valuation provides a look at how impoverished the Irish had become under the landlord system that had taken root in much of the South and West of Ireland. Some reform had been instituted with the Land Act of 1880. Additional advances were made with the Land Act of 1881, but the passage of the 1881 act came as a direct result of a wave of violence that became known as the Land War.

Chapter 5
The Land War (1879-1882)

Too long a sacrifice can make a stone of the heart.
William Butler Yeats

Even before the establishment of the Land League, parts of Ireland were ripe for civil unrest. As the number of evictions rose during the mini-famine of 1877-1879, so did the violence as noted in the *New York Herald*:

> In the collision which took place on Saturday at Knockrichard, County Mayo, several women were wounded with bayonets and swords. The men had incited them to resist the serving of processes [an increasingly popular tactic]. A large force of constabulary is now concentrated at Maam, County Galway, to protect the men who are to-day to serve ejectments over the property of the late Lord Leitrim. The people are reported to be decided to resort to extremities. The district is most excited and disturbed. The police and people are daily growing more exasperated with each other. (January 12, 1879)

The *Rochester Democrat and Chronicle* also reported on the violence in Maam: "There is little hope that bloodshed can be avoided as both parties are determined. Crowds are pouring in from the adjoining districts to resist eviction." (June 13, 1880)

Throughout the West, Land League rallies, known as monster meetings, were held, including one in Claremorris, Mayo, on April 20, 1879, led by Irish Nationalist James Daly, in which an estimated 20,000 people were in attendance, including most of the farmers from Mayo, Galway, and Roscommon. Many wore Land League cards in their hats while others wore green rosettes and medals. As the crowd waited for the speakers to mount the dais, they were entertained by a fife and drum band. It was at the Claremorris meeting that a policy of agitation took shape.

The labor government of Prime Minister Gladstone found this new development of mass meetings concerning. In response, in the summer of 1880, Gladstone introduced a bill that would ensure that a landlord would have to pay compensation to an evicted tenant for improvements made to his land and cottage during his tenancy. Although the Compensation for Disturbance Bill passed in the Commons, it was defeated in the House of Lords by a large majority. Its defeat acted as a match to a combustible Ireland.

Official statements from the Land League denouncing violence were undercut by the increase in agrarian crime throughout Ireland, but most particularly in the West and South. Many of these "outrages" were directed against those who violated a new policy of shunning and social ostracism against those who had evicted tenants or took possession of property from which tenants had been evicted. Parnell, in a speech in Ennis, stated that "a land grabber should be put into moral Coventry and isolated as if he was a leper of old." This moral Coventry was first used against the eponymous Captain Charles Boycott, land agent for Lord Erne, whose estate was located on Lough Mask, County Mayo.

Recognizing the devastating effects of the poor harvests of the late 1870s, Lord Erne had proposed a reduction in rent of ten percent. However, his tenants, backed by the Land League, demanded a twenty-five percent reduction. When Lord Erne refused to make additional adjustments, he ordered his agent to evict eleven tenants from their cottages. At the instigation of the Land League, Captain Boycott soon found himself in a world of trouble with his neighbors. According to the Parnell Commission of 1888:

> On the 22nd September, 1880, Captain Boycott's walls were thrown down, his cattle driven off, and scattered over the roads. He had no one to work for him, but had to do the work of the stables and farm himself. He could not get his horses shod, the smith telling him that he was very sorry, but that he dare not do it. He had to procure provisions through a friend from Cong, not being able to get them himself from Ballinrobe [the closest market town], where he usually obtained them. When he met the people on the road they hooted and booed at him and spat

across his feet as he went. In consequence of this treatment, he had to leave and went with his wife and family to the Harman Hotel at Dublin. They were not allowed to remain there, the landlord having received a threatening notice that if he kept them, it would be at his peril. Captain Boycott therefore left the country, and remained away for nearly twelve months. During his absence a steward whom he had left in charge employed a man named Michael Farragher, whereupon a shot was fired through Farragher's door. Captain Boycott returned in September, 1881, when he was again hooted and mobbed and his effigy hanged and burnt in the market square. He was obliged to have police protection. No cause for this treatment of Captain Boycott has been suggested other than his collecting rents.

James Bermingham, who enjoyed the double distinction of being a process-server and a tenant of an evicted farm, told a story of six years' steady boycotting from '81—a dreary interval enlivened occasionally by the destruction of his walls, by maimings of his sheep and cattle, by bullets coming through his windows.

What the tenants learned from their actions against Captain Boycott was that the tactic worked, and it spread throughout the country. For those who defied the boycott, houses were burned, cattle maimed, sheep drowned, dogs poisoned, and horses shot. Outrages against animals were followed by human mutilation: Ears were cropped, bodies singed, hair set on fire, and process-servers stoned.

As a result, in Galway during the Land War, there was a policeman for every forty-seven male adults and a soldier for every ninety-seven. It was only a matter of time before acts of violence against process servers escalated to targeted murder of a member of the landlord class, and the first victim would be Lord Mountmorres of Ebor Hall.

Chapter 6
Murder of Lord Mountmorres
September 25, 1880

"I do not know what will become of this unfortunate country."
From a letter written by Mountmorres on September 11, 1880
and published in the *Times* of London

Victim:
William Browne de Montmorency, Lord Mountmorres

Arrested:
Patrick Sweeney, Herdsman for Lord Mountmorres
Francis Gannon, Slater from Ballinrobe working in Clonbur
Patrick Hefferan, Plasterer working in Clonbur
William Spencer, Under-steward to Lord Ardilaun
Michael Burke, William Burke, John Hanberry
Patrick Hennelly, Arrested in England

Informer:
Michael Burke

Witnesses:
James Colgan, David Corbett

Police:
Head Constable Rudden
Sub-inspectors McArdle and Law

Magistrates:
A. Newton Brady, R. M.
M. Dennehy, R. M.
Mr. Blake, R. M.

Defense Counsel:
Charles O'Malley

Crown Prosecutor:
Mr. O'Farrell

Likely Culprits:
Patrick Kearney, Publican
Martin Fallon, Patrick Hennelly, Patrick Mulroe,
Thomas Murphy, Patrick Sweeney,
John/William Hanberry

William Browne de Montmorency, 5th Viscount Mountmorres, seemed an unlikely target for murder. After graduating from Trinity College with honors, William joined his father on the remote Montmorency estate of Tubbercurry in County Sligo where he was a "prime favorite with the peasants, who were loud in their praise of his good nature." Having taken some medical courses at Trinity, he "devoted himself to the amateur practice of medicine and was always ready to answer a 'sick call' at any hour, the country people deriving much comfort from medical attendance whose irregularity savored of the quackery so dear to the Irish peasant."

After marrying Harriet Broadrick of Hamphall Stubbs, Yorkshire, in 1862, Viscount Mountmorres used his wife's dowry to purchase Ebor Hall in Galway. Located about two and half miles from Clonbur, the house was of modest size for a lord but one with an excellent view of Tumneenaun Bay in Lough Corrib. It was reported that Mountmorres had paid double the value for the house and surrounding acres and was in a precarious financial position from the start. It is estimated that the Ebor Hall estate generated somewhere between £250 and £300 per annum. When that sum was combined with income from his other properties, Mountmorres had a net income of about £350 per annum *on paper*. But what was collected in rents rarely exceeded what was owed because, with the purchase of Ebor Hall, came eleven families of paupers who were almost always behind in their rent.

The murder occurred when Lord Mountmorres was returning home from a magistrates' meeting in Clonbur on Saturday evening,

September 25, 1880. During the meeting, a resolution had passed calling for the Government to take coercive measures to quell the growing violence throughout Ireland, including the threat of violence that existed within its own jurisdiction. It is estimated that Mountmorres left the magistrates' meeting at about 7:00. Two witnesses, Sub-inspector W. B. Law and Head Constable Timothy O'Callaghan, stated that they had had a conversation with Mountmorres at that time concerning security arrangements for a Land League meeting the next day in Clonbur and that he had had no police protection for the last three months. The reason given for the lack of a police escort was that on a prior occasion, one of the constables assigned to His Lordship was inebriated. His decision to forgo police protection is a curious one considering the state of unrest then existing in the region.[13]

After his discussions with the inspector and constable, Mountmorres traveled south along the main road from Clonbur to his estate on Lough Corrib in his jaunting car. At that time of year, sunset would have been at about 7:30, approximately the time Mountmorres was on the road to Ebor Hall. He was about a mile from his home when he was ambushed.

The numerous tributes that followed Mountmorres's murder described him as a thick-set man, five-foot, seven inches:

> ...whose dress betrayed no symptom of care or neatness; his grizzly hair and beard added at least ten years to his age and a general want of firmness in his gait seemed to indicate that he was more than forty-eight. His first care in the morning was to feed the fowl; his next to look after his black retrievers, of which he was very proud. During the day he walked about the small farm or drove after luncheon into the village of Clonbur or Maam, conversing with the peasants on terms of most

---

[13] During an appearance before J. A. Bryne, Q. C. in Ballinrobe in connection with a claim for compensation for her husband's death under The Prevention of Crimes Act, Lord Mountmorres's widow stated that shortly before her husband's murder, they had attended a ball at Ashford House as guests of Lord and Lady Ardilaun. On the way to Ebor Hall, they were stopped by a stranger and warned not to go home through a plantation located near a quarry but rather to go home by a longer route, which they did. (It sounds almost biblical.)

perfect equality... Living a life of such rigid simplicity, thrown upon the society of the peasants—for neighbors he had none—and apparently enjoyed their society on terms equally, it might be assumed that Lord Mountmorres was, if any person in the position of gentleman could be, a favorite with the people... His social enjoyments were greatly restricted by his poverty, and his refusal of an abatement of rent was to him a positive necessity.

Trouble first appeared on the horizon of Ebor Hall in 1877 with the onset of the mini-famine. Although 1878 was a little better than the previous year, 1879 proved to be a disaster for every tenant in the "wet West." When rents came due, not one of Mountmorres tenants was in a position to pay the full rent, and they asked for a reduction of thirty percent. When their landlord countered with a less generous offer of twenty percent, relations became strained.[14]

If Mountmorres had once been "a favourite of the people," the Land War and a three-year famine had changed that. In addition to receiving threatening notices, on his property, he found sheep drowned in the lake and a heifer abandoned in a deep soft pond in the field, and he believed that the acts were malicious, which, undoubtedly, they were, and Mountmorres had succeeded in obtaining compensation for malicious injuries to his animals.

Despite rising tensions between landlord and tenants, Lord Mountmorres was not Lord Leitrim. Although he had sent out processes of ejectment, he had not actually evicted any tenant, and even though it was believed that he was separated from his wife (who was in Scotland at the time of his death), the debauchery attributed to the Donegal lord did not gain traction with Mountmorres despite the efforts of his opponents to paint him with the same brush as Lord Leitrim. But if the cause of His Lordship's murder was not seducing the local virgins or evicting tenants, other reasons for waylaying the viscount had to exist. Although officials of the Land League, through regular and vigorous pronouncements, continued to distance themselves from the violence their movement had unleashed, it was

---

[14] The average reduction of rents fixed in the land courts established by the 1881 Land Act was 19.5%. Lord Mountmorres had offered twenty percent and had been refused.

difficult to separate the two as indicated in this editorial from the *Times* of London:

> Lord Mountmorres had a very small property and could not afford like other landlords to have his rental cut off, or even seriously cut down. He had been obliged to resort to legal measures to bring some tenants to terms, and this aroused the vindictive spirit which the agitators had created... It is in vain that the land agitators now repudiate all responsibility for the crime and speak of it in terms or horror. Let them unteach if they can the lessons of the last 18 months they have been impressing upon an ignorant and excitable people... Let them endeavor to revive the principles of honesty and the instincts of humanity which they have helped to stifle by appeals to the base passions of cupidity and revenge. They may then hope to get some credit for at least sincere repentance and an earnest desire to lead the misguided people back into the paths of reason and justice.

In response to the outrage expressed in the *Times*, the leaders of the Land League continued to dispute a connection between Lord Mountmorres's death and agrarian agitation. Instead, they pointed to the murdered lord's suspected role as an informer for the British Government as the primary cause for his death, but there were other reasons as well.

As was common practice in rural Ireland, a landlord very often served as a magistrate at the petty sessions. The majority of minor disputes, both criminal and civil, such as unpaid debts, trespass, drunk and disorderly, assault, etc., were heard by this court.[15] The magistrates often had no legal training and rendered judgment at the time of the hearing. Those who lauded the murdered lord declared: "In all complaints at the suit of the police or other authorities he was looked upon as the people's magistrate, and his voice could be counted upon in opposition to what less tender-hearted men would call stern justice." But others did not see him in so bright a light as noted in *Donohoe's Monthly Journal*:

---

[15] Crimes of a more serious nature, those requiring a jury, were held at the Quarter Sessions. Capital offenses were presided over by at least one legally trained judge at the assizes held twice a year in circuit.

As a magistrate he was a ferocious partisan. He was continually displaying his partisanship on the benches of all the neighboring courts of petty sessions. He was continually in litigation with his neighbors, summoning them for unintentional acts of trespass, to which any other person would have paid no regard whatever. He sometimes, it is said, went so far as to sit in judgment in cases in which he was personally concerned. Only a few weeks since he, as a magistrate sitting at Maam, gave a decision requiring some persons to pay poor-rates, although they were rated under £4, and were therefore exempted from the tax by the Land Act of 1870.

American James Redpath, at that time a special correspondent for the *Inter Ocean* newspaper of Chicago, had been touring the area the week before the Mountmorres murder in preparation for a speech he was to give on September 26th at the Land League meeting in Clonbur. In his "Talks about Ireland," Redpath noted that "as I was working it [his speech] out in my mind, a citizen of the place joined me. One after another, seven or eight outside cars passed me on their way to the constabulary headquarters. Each jaunting-car had four armed constables on it. I asked why they were coming. 'Oh, don't you know the Government has sent down a short-hand writer to report your speech to-morrow, and these constables are here to protect him.'" The "citizen," dressed in light clothing, who spoke to Redpath was Lord Mountmorres.

While driving about the country with Father Watt Conway, a curate in Clonbur parish, Redpath noted parcels of oats with all the heads gone and asked about a "field of standing straw." Father Conway explained that the field belonged to Lord Mountmorres and that "he cannot get a man to cut his oats or work on his farm for love or money…this in a parish where men are eager to get work." Nor would his tenants harvest his potatoes, and only "the peasant women of the house were left to save them." The priest shared with Redpath that Mountmorres had reported a man for "pulling a few handfuls of furze, and he was heavily fined for it."[16]

---

[16] Furze, a prolific plant with a yellow flower, also known as gorse, grows like a weed across the West of Ireland and was used to get a peat fire going. Today, farmers regard it as a nuisance. Permitted burns take place between September and February.

Father Conway further explained that Mountmorres had "made himself very obnoxious to the people by his capricious decisions as a magistrate...whoever sent him a jug of whisky or a fat turkey was sure to have a verdict in his favor." But even more damning than Mountmorres's bought favors and biased decisions was Father Conway's contention that it was "generally believed that he was constantly sending bad reports to [Dublin] Castle," the home of the Lord Lieutenant, and a symbol of an oppressive British presence in an occupied Ireland.

After the assassination, Redpath reported that Mountmorres was known locally as a "wet soul—[or] in America as a barroom loafer." Clonbur residents told the correspondent that Mountmorres, although a lord, "frequented all the barrooms of the village and drank at the expense of and in the company of any one who chose to treat him...," including "the vilest characters in the meanest public houses." He was known to brag about how he would make "the best detective," sussing out information to share with his fellow proprietors.

Redpath was told that His Lordship "had fallen from his car more than once, and his horse had made more than one solitary journey" to Ebor Hall, at which time, his servants would go in search of their drunken master. Redpath, himself, had seen Mountmorres in his jaunting car "so drunk that he could hardly sit in the car."

Other problems arose with Patrick Sweeney, a herdsman for Lord Mountmorres, who lived in a cottage that went with the position. Sweeney is a good example of the confusion generated by the Land Act of 1870. When Lord Mountmorres attempted to remove the herdsman for non-payment of rent,[17] Sweeney claimed the status of tenant, and litigation ensued. However, at the Quarter Sessions, the magistrates ruled in favor of Mountmorres, a fellow magistrate. A month after that decision, His Lordship requested police protection from the constabulary. A year later, Mountmorres settled with Sweeney, allowing him to stay on the farm and in the cottage. An uneasy peace followed, but it did not last.

Head Constable Rudden, described by the *Guardian* as a "burly,

---

[17] Father Conway stated that Sweeney paid his rent with his labor as Mountmorres's herd.

square-headed, Irish police type," who investigated the murder, later testified before the Parnell Commission in 1888 that he attributed Mountmorres's unpopularity to the fact that he made no secret of his opposition to the Land League and that he openly spoke about the need for the Government to suppress League activities. He also had a reputation for sending men to prison for minor offenses.

Fuel was added to the fire when, in the spring of 1880, Mountmorres was returning from Dublin when he saw a man emerge from the woods carrying wood that belonged to one of his neighbors. Instead of talking to the man, the viscount reported the illegal cutting to the owner of the woods, and when the man appeared at the petty sessions to answer to the charge, Lord Mountmorres acted as a witness against him. The man was fined ten shillings (one-half pound)—an enormous sum when one considers that most of His Lordship's tenants were too poor to pay the poor rate based on a yearly income of less than four pounds.

The effect of his interference was immediate. "Lord Mountmorres was reviled as an informer. His own tenants, who had paid him no rent, now refused to do any work for him, and the small crop of oats sown in the spring stood until it was eaten by cattle, as no one could be got to cut it... Still the mere fact of telling a neighbor's caretaker that the former's woods were being broken down has not hitherto been considered sufficient to place a man's life in danger, and though Lord Mountmorres was again offered the protection of the police, he declined it."

But the question remains: Were Mountmorres's actions sufficient cause to ambush and kill him? A clue of what might have been the real reason for the assassination was provided in a speech given at a Land League meeting on November 2, 1880, five weeks after Mountmorres' death, by American newspaperman James Redpath, whose sympathies aligned with the tenants in the Land War: "The friends of the Irish peasantry had been altogether too gentle in their talk about their infamous rascal. He *was* a Government spy, and once bragged that he was in the pay of the Castle." In his testimony before the Parnell Commission, Head Constable Rudden confirmed that it was a widely held belief that Mountmorres *was* being paid by Dublin Castle. Considering Mountmorres's precarious financial situation, it is reasonable to think that he sought payment from the Government in exchange for information.

If it was believed that Mountmorres was, in fact, a Government spy, that alone would have been sufficient cause for someone to take lethal action against him. The possibility exists that once the land agitation began, Lord Mountmorres, who was known to bend an elbow at Patrick Kearney's public house in Clonbur, may have made use of information he had gleaned from over-listening conversations as Kearney's was a meeting place for Land League agitators. Testimony given during the Parnell Commission inferred that the viscount's murder was plotted in Kearney's pub.[18]

A laborer named John Burke was the first person who saw the body. At the inquest, Burke stated that:

> On Saturday he had been in Clonbur, and had seen Lord Mountmorres there... Witness passed on the road what he thought was a drunken man [lying in the road]. On arriving at home, he told some friends, and, so as to prevent the man being killed by a car passing over him, they started to go down and lift him up, but on their way, they met an old woman, the old nurse of Lord Mountmorres, who said his Lordship was lying on the road, and that his car had come home empty. She asked them to come down and remove him to his residence. They said they would willingly carry him home on their backs, but that if they went down by themselves he might shoot them in a mistake with the revolver he carried. They accordingly refused to go unless the old woman accompanied them; but as she declined to do so they did not go to his Lordship's assistance.[19]

According to the *Inter Ocean*, the nurse then went on to Clonbur to get help.

After being notified that His Lordship's horse and carriage had arrived at Ebor Hall without him, Sub-inspector Law sent a message to

---

[18] Barbara Ann Kearney, great-great-granddaughter of Patrick Kearney, shared with the author that her great-great-grandfather, a Galway farmer and publican, was a colonel, aka a "centre," in a clandestine Fenian organization. Later, he served as regional treasurer and secretary for the Land League.

[19] When His Lordship's horse and empty carriage arrived at Ebor Hall, the nurse assumed Mountmorres was drunk and set out to bring him home.

the barracks in Clonbur, and an immediate search was undertaken. The body of Lord Mountmorres was found in Dooroy, about a mile from his house, lying face up across the road from Clonbur in a pool of blood. He had been shot six times. A loaded pistol was found in his pocket, a lantern was located near the body, and a bottle of whisky was found in the well of his carriage. A watch and about two pounds were also found on the body, ruling out robbery as a motive. It was determined that he had been shot from two revolvers as two of the bullets recovered from Mountmorres's body were from different molds.[20]

Ebor Hall, Flanagan Cottage, Jaunting Car
on road south from Clonbur Road

Dr. John Hegarty, a medical officer at the Clonbur dispensary who "attended the constabulary barracks," was sent for at 10:00 p.m. and arrived at approximately 11:00 p.m. After Dr. Hegarty thought he had detected a pulse, instructions were given to take Lord Mountmorres to the nearest home—that of Hugh Flanagan. Flanagan was awakened by someone banging on his door. He was asked to take the body into his home but refused. When he appeared to waver, his wife and daughters

---

[20] According to Professor Pat Finnegan, in nearby Tuam, "rifles and revolvers were offered for sale openly," and there were plenty to be had. *Loughrea, 'That Den of Infamy,' The Land War in Co. Galway, 1879-1882*, p. 67.

came down from an upstairs room in their night clothes and blocked the doorway. Flanagan also refused to allow the body to be taken to an out-building, and so it was that Lord Mountmorres remained in the Flanagan yard until such time as arrangements could be made for a car to take him to his home. Flanagan did provide "a lamp and some fire" for the ride to Ebor Hall.

With the assistance of "two civilians," the body was taken to the Mountmorres residence. Once at the hall, the body was locked in the coachhouse.

Hugh Flanagan's refusal to allow the constables to carry Lord Mountmorres's body into the house may seem heartless, but it was in keeping with centuries-old superstitions regarding interactions with the dead and its consequences. As Flanagan stated: "Nothing belonging to me would be alive that day twelve months" as a result of violating societal taboos. There were also political consequences to be considered. Although the term "boycott" was not then in general use, the concept was already being applied to anyone who cooperated with the authorities or took the landlord's side in tenant disputes, and Lord Mountmorres was, after all, a landlord.

At Ebor Hall, an examination was undertaken by Dr. Hegarty. It was found that there was one bullet to the forehead, two in the neck, two in the abdomen, and one in the right thumb. Powder residue was found in the eyebrows, indicating that the bullet had been fired from a short distance. Later, a post-mortem, conducted by Dr. Maguire of Cong and Dr. O'Connor of Oughterard, determined that "the wound in the forehead was quite sufficient to cause death."

An inquest was held on the evening of September 27, 1880 in the study of Ebor Hall by Mr. C. G. Cottingham, Coroner. Those present included Lord Ardilaun, Reverend M. Dockery, County Inspector Cullen, Mr. M. Dennehy, R. M. [resident magistrate], Mr. Blake, R. M., and Sub-inspectors McArdle and Law.[21] Also in attendance were two

---

[21] In pre-independence Ireland, a Resident Magistrate was a stipendiary magistrate appointed by the Lord Lieutenant to sit among justices of the peace at the petty sessions in that county. RMs did not need to be legally trained, and many were ex-British Army officers. "Resident" referred to the requirement that the magistrate live in the county to which he was assigned. The role was often criticized for being under the influence of Dublin Castle. (Wikipedia – "Resident Magistrate")

brothers of the deceased, Hon. Francis de Montmorency and Hon. Arthur Hill Trevor de Montmorency. After examining the extensive wounds on the body, the coroner's jury returned a verdict of "willful murder against person or persons unknown."

Suspicion immediately fell on Patrick Sweeney, who was then under notice to quit the farm. (Mountmorres's solicitor in Tuam had received instructions to serve Sweeney with an ejectment decree.) The ejectment notice was sufficient to order his arrest "on suspicion," and he was taken into custody on September 28, 1880 and appeared at the Galway Quarter Sessions on October 1st before Magistrate Dennehy.[22]

Father Watt Conway, the parish priest at Clonbur, came to Sweeney's defense—somewhat:

> 'I could have believed that Sweeney would have been capable of murdering him with a stick, but, poor man, I know he is in no way versed in the use of a rifle, and, without a doubt, a rifle was used in this case. [Revolvers were used.] Then again, he is a simple-minded man, while the spot selected for the commission of this crime indicates a well-learnt lesson. You will see from the pool of blood that the deceased fell at the brow of a steep hill; his horse, whatever its powers, must necessarily have walked up the hill. Thus the murder must have been planned to be perpetrated while the horse was going at a walking pace, and without doubt while the deceased was off his guard.' Father Conway insisted that he could not believe for a moment that any local resident had committed so diabolical a crime.

Francis Gannon, a slater from Ballinrobe, who happened to be working on a house in Clonbur for the previous three weeks, was also arrested as it was believed that years earlier, he had been a member of the Fenians and had been heard to say in a public house that "the fate of Lord Mountmorres was only what bad landlords and magistrates

---

[22] At his hearing in Clonbur for remand, Patrick Sweeney was described as "an infirm man, apparently verging on 70 years of age" (more likely fifty) and "seemed dejected." ("The Agitation in Ireland – The Murder of Lord Mountmorres – Examination of the Accused," *Guardian* (Manchester), October 2, 1880.

had to expect." When questioned, he was "shaking like a leaf," and that drew the suspicion of the police.

Francis Gannon had nothing to do with Mountmorres's murder. The police, in their haste to arrest someone, disregarded multiple witnesses who were prepared to swear that Gannon had been in their company at the time of the murder. As a result, the slater was remanded and then remanded again. At one of the hearings, as reported in the *Times*, Gannon stated: "I can get plenty of evidence that I did not leave the place that day or night. I have 30 to prove it in this town, and I do not see why I should be detained eight days from my work." His wife agreed and shouted to the magistrate, "and from his wife and family, too." (October 2, 1880)

On October 11th, Patrick Heffernan, a plasterer, and William Spencer, under-steward to Lord Ardilaun, were arrested. Spencer, a married man who was arrested at midnight and taken from his bed, had been, on the evening of Mountmorres's murder, drinking at a Clonbur public house. The reason for the arrest was that Spencer and his party had left the pub at about the same time as His Lordship was leaving Clonbur and had proceeded in the direction of Ebor Hall. Spencer was unpopular, and his unpopularity may have been a result of his position as Lord Ardilaun's under-steward, and for that reason, he carried a revolver.[23]

On October 15th, the four prisoners were brought to the courthouse at Cong with an escort of twenty armed constables and charged with complicity in the murder of Lord Mountmorres. The men were brought before Mr. Dennehy, the resident magistrate at Oughterard, who had been specially directed by the Government to attend the proceedings at Cong and assist the police with his advice.[24]

James Colgan, a stock manager to Richard Berridge, a non-resident Galway landlord, was the only witness called by the Crown. According to Colgan, he had been in Clonbur on September 25th. He left the

---

[23] William Spencer, an Englishman, eventually became head steward at Ashford House and lived at the estate until his death in 1920. He is buried on the Castle grounds. www.maggieblanck.com, "Land Issues, Murder of Lord Mountmorres."

[24] Today, the Cong Courthouse is the local tourist board and is within easy walking distance of the medieval Cong Abbey. The entire building is about 600 square feet.

village to return to his home at about 7:00. Travelling with him in a side car were William Spencer and two men named Walsh.

As he approached the spot in the road where Mountmorres was shot, Colgan met two men coming in the opposite direction. When asked by Crown Prosecutor O'Farrell if he had seen the men since that time, Colgan said that he hadn't. At the crossroads, about 140 yards from where Mountmorres was killed, Colgan had stopped the car to let Spencer out. It was at that time that Spencer shared with Colgan that he had received threats against his life and that "he would be shot." Spencer had bragged to Colgan: "I would like to see the man who would do it." At that point, he took out a revolver and fired two shots. Colgan testified that due to the lay of the land, it was impossible for the bullets fired by Spencer to have killed Mountmorres.

After the examination was finished, the Crown's case collapsed, and Mr. O'Farrell declared that it was not in the public's interest to continue, stating that the possibility existed that "the Crown will obtain satisfactory information at another time." Charles O'Malley, counsel for the prisoners, asked that the prisoners be discharged, and R. M. Dennehy ordered their release.

In December 1880, three men, Michael Burke, William Burke, and John/William Hanberry, were arrested in Clonbur on suspicion of complicity in the murder of Lord Mountmorres. Following their arrests, the police searched the home of a butcher named Hennelly in Dooray, whose house was near the scene of the murder, and removed a letter sent by Hennelly's son, who was away from home. And this is where the plot thickens. In the town of Tipton, in the English Midlands, Patrick Hennelly, 37, the butcher's son, was arrested. His description fit that of a man who had recently shot an Irish laborer named Gateley at Solihill near Birmingham "in compliance with the order of a secret society." Upon searching his rooms in Tipton, a letter from Hennelly's mother was found, but the police admitted that "it contained nothing to criminate the prisoner," and its only purpose was to establish Hennelly's identity after Hennelly had refused to provide that information to the police. A constable conducting the search was heard to say that "if they didn't get Hennelly for Mountmorres's murder, they would get him for the laborer's."[25] It would be reasonable to assume that Hennelly was in the North of England, and not in Clonbur, at the time of the Mountmorres murder—an assumption that would prove to be wrong.

On January 27, 1881, Michael Burke, Patrick Hennelly, and John/William Hanberry were charged with being concerned in His Lordship's murder.[26] On that day, Thomas Hogan, a laborer who had been working alongside the son of the accused Michael Burke in Kylebeg near Clonbur, testified that he had seen Michael Burke, Patrick Hennelly, and William Burke in Kearney's club on the night of the murder.

It was also on that day that David Corbett, a boy of about ten from the village of Tumneenaum, southwest of Dooroy, stated that he had been in Clonbur with his father and brother on September 25th and had seen Lord Mountmorres at the post office with his pony and car and knew the pony well. According to the *Guardian*:

> Witness lived about a quarter of a mile beyond Ebor Hall. He followed his Lordship in a car and got on the axle. He remained on the axle until the car was stopped on the road by two or three men. He could not say as it was so dark, whether there were two or three men. They caught hold of Lord Mountmorres and pulled him off the car. His Lordship said to them, "Who is that? Are you going to kill me?" Witness got off the axle and ran away. He heard five or six shots. He ran home, and on the way, met a man with a cart of turf. He found his mother, sister, and a boy named Patrick Molloy in his parents' house when he got home, but did not say anything about the murder until the boy

---

[25] Hennelly, a former "road worker" on Lord Ardilaun's estate, left Dooroy six months prior to his arrest in connection with the Mountmorres murder for Tipton in the North of England where his brother Michael lived—a fact acknowledged by the police in England. Regarding the Irish laborer killed near Birmingham, a boy who had witnessed the murder failed to identify Hennelly in an identity parade "as the man he saw running away after Gateley was shot."

[26] "Hanberry could not be brought from the barrack [to the Clonbur Courthouse], as he is suffering from a fracture of the skull." "The Murder of Lord Mountmorres," *Guardian*, January 5, 1881. No information was given as to how Hanberry came to have a cracked skull; however, Dr. John Hegarty, his physician, stated that the man was able to walk around the yard of the Clonbur barracks despite his injury.

had gone. He did not call at the gatehouse at Ebor hall… It was so dark that he could not distinguish the features of the men who pulled Lord Mountmorres from the car. He would not know *either* of them again.[27]

The boy's testimony is most likely the closest to the truth we will ever get. On the evening of September 25th, it was known that Lord Mountmorres was to attend a magistrates' meeting in Clonbur and that he would return to Ebor Hall after the meeting had ended. While His Lordship was in Clonbur, two or three men moved into position and waited at the top of a rise in the road. Riding in an open car, and seeing the men in the road, Mountmorres slowed his horse and quickly realized it was an ambush. The number of shots heard by David Corbett corresponds to the number of bullet wounds found on Mountmorres's body.

Nothing came of these arrests, and Patrick Sweeney was soon seen driving cattle into the Ballinrobe market as he had done before Lord Mountmorres's murder. Even with the collapse of the Crown's case, the local populace remained in a state of agitation, and the constabulary, housed in police huts, patrolled the whole of the district.

Land League activists and local clergy continued to deny that the Land League had any hand in the death of Lord Mountmorres. While they protested, threatening letters, signed "Rory" and "Moonlight," were mailed to those who stood in opposition to the Land League, several stating that they would meet the same fate as Mountmorres if their opposition continued. A reward of £1,000, from W. E. Forster, Lord Lieutenant of Ireland, for information leading to the arrest and conviction of the killers went unclaimed even though a free pardon was attached to the offer.

Even though no one was ever convicted of the crime, there were many who believed that Lord Mountmorres's murder had been ordered by the Land League. Some of the blame for this must fall on questionable public-relations decisions by Land League officials. In County Wexford, on the day after the murder, Charles Stewart Parnell

---

[27] According to a descendant of David Corbett, David was taken out on Lough Corrib by the police and threatened with drowning if he did not reveal the names of Mountmorres's killers. Despite the threats, David insisted that it was too dark to know who they were. The Corbett family remains on the property.

had refused to condemn the killing, blaming the assassination on England's policies in Ireland.

The most likely suspects emerged during testimony before a special Parliamentary commission investigating Parnellism and Crime in 1888. At that time, a laborer named Michael Burke was called to testify in connection with the assassination of Lord Mountmorres. Eight years earlier, Burke had joined a secret society in Jarrow, England, a mining and ship-building center on the River Tyne. According to his testimony, while in Ireland, he had attended secret-society meetings at Cong, Rusheen, Clonbur, and Tourmakeady. In Clonbur, meetings were held in the house or in the backyard of the publichouse of publican Patrick Kearney.

On November 22, 1889, the *Times* of London printed a transcript of Michael Burke's testimony:

> A fortnight after I was working at a place called Kylebeg, belonging to Lord Ardilaun, about a mile from Clonbur, we were in a field a bit from the road. I saw Sweeney coming from the road... He called me aside a little to him and asked me if I would assist that evening to do away with Lord Mountmorres. I said I would but I had a wife and family to look after, and I might only for that.
>
> Afterwards, between 12 and 1 o'clock, Pat Mulroe came. He did not say much, but he said he expected Lord Mountmorres was going to be done away with that evening... At 6 o'clock I left work and went to Kearney's publichouse. I saw Kearney, Sweeney, Barrett, Martin Fallon, Thomas Murphy, William Hansbury [sic], Pat Henilly [sic], William Burke—a house full of them...
>
> Pat Sweeney asked me at the door if I was going to lend a hand to murder—to do away with Lord Mountmorres... I gave consent to Kearney. He told me I would be better to go along with the rest and lend them a hand. I missed some of them—Sweeney, Mulroe, Fallon, I think, Thomas Murphy—after that. I think Kearney went out, and I was inclined to go, but I met Kearney on the return at the door, and he told me to return back, that it was too late, so I turned into the publichouse and remained there.

About half-past 8, Pat Mulroe came back. I see some of the wounds on his hand, but I cannot say what it was. I went some little way with him on the way home. He said that they had done away with Lord Mountmorres.

Sir Charles Russell, a supporter of land reform, whose purpose before the Commission was to show that a series of murders was in no way connected with the Land League, attempted to pin on Michael Burke the label of informer—someone not truly honorable—who worked on the fringes of Land League activity in Clonbur.[28] According to Russell, although Burke knew Mountmorres was marked for murder, he did nothing to warn His Lordship nor did he take part in the actual murder. He used Burke's own words to neutralize his testimony:

> "I [Michael Burke] do not know the society I joined. I cannot name any others who were along with me… I cannot say who asked me to attend the Land League. I attended a few meetings, but I cannot say where they were. I will not swear the meetings were at Kearney's. I will not swear whether they were Land League meetings or not…[or if] there was a Land League at Clonbur at that time."

Although no one was ever successfully prosecuted for the murder of Lord Mountmorres, nevertheless, Michael Burke's testimony is compelling as it appears likely that the men named by Burke either committed the murder or were accessories to murder, including Patrick Hennelly who was in Clonbur, and not in England, on the night of Mountmorres's murder.

In the days immediately after Lord Mountmorres's assassination, there were reports of several men who were seen dancing in the blood of the victim. During the hearings on Parnellism and Crime, Sergeant O'Connor of the Royal Irish Constabulary, who was assigned to the Clonbur Barracks, testified that after a Land League meeting in Clonbur, he went to the place where His Lordship had been killed:

---

[28] Charles Russell (Baron Russell of Killowen) was elected member of parliament for Hackney South (1885–1894). He was knighted and appointed Attorney General by Prime Minister William Ewart Gladstone in 1886 and again in 1892 on the return of the Liberals to power.

"There were marks of blood on the ground... There were five persons—men—there... They were jumping and shouting in a circle with their hands joined... They ran away before I got up to them."

There is something in the savagery of that scene that evokes an image of a people who had snapped. They lived in squalid cottages, eking out a living from an impoverished soil, with despair a constant companion. Although Lord Mountmorres was hardly the cartoon image of a landlord cracking the whip and charging rack-rents, he had become the embodiment of centuries of oppression at a time when there existed a glimmer of hope that change was possible. The Land League had thrown them a lifeline, and a repressed tenantry had grabbed on to it with gusto.

The violence in Galway and Mayo was such that by June 1880, "Parnell and Davitt were to admit that they had 'lost Mayo' [as] Secret Societies had taken over..." Davitt stated that the area of Mayo and Galway from Claremorris, through Hollymount, The Neale, Ballinrobe and out to Clonbur was a "veritable storm centre, a flashpoint, during the Land War... As militant Mayo thought, so thought they." After a lifetime of living under the thumbs of their oppressors, their search for redress had turned violent.

In England, as evidenced by articles appearing in the *Times* of London, among certain classes, there was outrage over the murder of the Irish peer:

> [His murder] excited feelings of alarm little short of actual panic among all the respectable classes irrespective of politics or creed... Although at present the panic which prevails is felt most keenly by those who have any relations with landed property, it is shared by others who are employers of labour and see the growth of a refractory and ruthless spirit among the subordinate classes... The people...listen to incessant denunciations of landlords as rapacious tyrants who had secured the land and held it by no moral right, but by legalized robbery, supported by the brute force of an alien Government...With such ideas of the landlord class dinned into their ears, is it to be wondered at that they are quite ready to revenge any injury, real or imaginary, which they may receive, and think it no crime, but rather a meritorious action to rid society of one of the hated species when an opportunity occurs?"

In America, there was a different take of what had happened in Ireland, and the *Brooklyn Daily Eagle*, spoke for many Irish-Americans when it wrote:

> Our esteemed contemporaries of the English press...view with feelings of the profoundest consternation the assassination of Lord Mountmorres, who was killed, doubtless by some of his evicted tenants. They declare that this act has produced alarm amounting almost to a panic, and their general tone seems to intimate that in their opinion civilization and progress have been brought up with a round turn...and the end of all things has been materially hastened by this unparalleled crime... Many of them were equally moved to despair...at the murder of one Lord Leitrim not very long ago. Between these two homicidal acts there have been plenty of murders in England as well as in Ireland, but it is significant that not one of these, cruel and unprovoked as some of them were, so painfully affected our esteemed contemporaries. We are therefore forced to the conclusion that the feeling of alarm...follows upon the fact that the victim of this murder was a lord and landholder, and that the sacrilegiousness, not the criminality, of the murder is what appalls and dismays them... Peasants by the score may be starved deliberately to the death to provide landlords with champagne and kid gloves, without shaking a nerve, but if a lord and a landowner comes to his end by violence...all nature is shaken to its foundation with horror and amazement.
>
> The average American will deprecate the murder of lords as a solution of difficulties between landlords and tenants, but he will also deprecate the difficulties and the selfish spirit which engendered them. He will, perhaps, observe that a man who is doomed to death by starvation will not be particular about the form in which death comes to him, whether through hunger or the hangman... Surely, the right to live is not the exclusive privilege of landowners, and if the law is to be enforced against murder in one form, it ought not to connive at the same crime in another. The world will not pause on its axis because Lord Leitrim and Lord Mountmorres have been murdered; other lords, however, may be induced by this startling *argumentum ad hominem* to pause and reflect before proceeding to extremities.

The British Government did not pause to reflect. On January 24, 1881, W. E. Forster, Chief Secretary for Ireland, introduced a new Coercion Bill in the House of Commons to deal with the violence in Ireland. Despite a forty-one-hour-long filibuster in the House by the Irish Parliamentary Party, the bill passed. Among its provisions was the right to arrest without trial persons who were reasonably suspected of crime and conspiracy. That provision would greatly impact the outcome of the murders of two agents of Lord Ardilaun in Galway's Murderer's Country.

Chapter 7
Arthur Guinness
1st Baron Ardilaun

In 1848, in the depths of the Great Famine, the Encumbered Estates Act was passed by the British Parliament for the purpose of facilitating the sale of Irish estates whose owners were unable to meet their financial obligations. It was hoped that the act would attract English investors and their capital as a way of improving and modernizing Irish agriculture. Unfortunately, the act provided no protection to the tenants living on the encumbered estates. In many cases, the estates were cleared of all existing tenants, their houses and outbuildings demolished, and their land turned over to the grazing of sheep or cattle. "Between 1849 and 1857, there were approximately 3,000 estates with a total area of 5,000,000 acres that were disposed of under the act. Many, but certainly not all, of the landlords were absentee, employing an agent to run the estate. The agent was often a person with a military background, was well paid and comfortably accommodated."

According to the National University of Ireland Connacht and Munster Landed Estates Database, in 1852, Sir Benjamin Lee Guinness, 1st Baronet (1798-1868), an heir to the Guinness brewery fortune, "acquired several Connaught estates that were up for sale in the Encumbered Estates' Court. He bought the Ashford estate from Lord Oranmore and Browne, the Doon estate from Sir Richard  O'Donnell, the Cong estate from Alexander Lambert, part of the Rosshill estate from the 3rd Lord Leitrim, parts of Connemara from Christopher St George. In 1859, he bought Kylemore from a banking consortium. With these purchases, Benjamin Guinness became landlord to 670 tenants, 316 of whom rented at less than £5 per annum."

With his father's death in 1868, Arthur Guinness, 2nd Baronet and oldest son and heir (1840-1915), continued in his father's footsteps, purchasing vast swaths of Galway, including, in 1871, the Elwood estate of Strandhill, just across the river from Ashford, Cong, the Inishdoorus islands on Lough Corrib, and lands in the barony of Ross near Cong in 1875.[29]

Arthur soon embarked on a lifetime program of improvements to the magnificent Ashford House (later renamed Ashford Castle). In addition to the house (at right), he built roads, drained bogs, planted thousands of trees, and subsidized a steamer that ran between Galway Bay and Lough Corrib. The property featured a two-hundred-acre park with manicured lawns and formal gardens. When Arthur's acquisitions were combined with those of his father, the total acreage for the Ashford estate was 33,298 with the result that Lord Ardilaun owned most of County Galway between Maam Bridge and Lough Mask.

But in assembling so large an estate, tenants were displaced, and many did not go quietly thinking as much of their cottage as Lord Ardilaun did of his castle:

> Lord Ardilaun encountered the same difficulties as other landlords who have endeavoured to increase the size of their smaller holdings and provide better dwellings for their people. Those bought out of small farms, miserably inadequate to provide a livelihood, talk as if they had been dispossessed of a

---

[29] Ardilaun's tenants included my great-great-grandparents, Catherine Varelley and John Lydon of Glenlusk. With John's passing in 1875, the year Ardilaun purchased the remainder of the Barony of Ross properties, the family—mother, daughter, and three sons—immigrated to the United States. It is possible that Ardilaun assisted in their emigration in order to remove pauper tenants from his property. If Ardilaun wanted to clear the land of debtor tenants, this was the time to do it.

magnificent inheritance without requital. Although liberal terms were given for disturbance, although payments were made for tenants' improvements, and good houses and farms were provided elsewhere, the clearing away small holders to make Ashford-park has caused considerable heartburning... Notwithstanding extended farms and better dwellings, some of the tenantry are by no means satisfied with their altered position. There is a manifest disposition to magnify the value of what has been given up and to underestimate what has been acquired.

Another example of His Lordship's failure to understand his Catholic tenants was a school he built for the children of his tenants at Ashford. Unfortunately, the schoolmaster, although a first-rate master, was a Protestant. This should not have mattered because, as part of the National School program, there was no religious teaching or proselytizing in the schools. But it did matter to a peasantry whose common bond was their Roman Catholic faith with all its attendant rites and rituals. Ardilaun's Catholic tenants preferred to send their children to school in Cong, three miles distant, where they would receive instruction from a Catholic master.

Despite considerable grumbling from Ardilaun's tenants, the expansion and improvement of Ashford House provided employment for between 400 and 500 artisans and laborers. Without this employment, many of the men would have migrated to England for seasonal work on farms or in the forges of the Midlands or the potato harvest in Scotland. Others might have chosen to go farther—to the United States, Canada, and Australia—never to return to Ireland.

In 1876, Arthur withdrew from the Guinness family business when he sold his half-share to his brother Edward for £600,000. In 1880, he was raised to the peerage as Baron Ardilaun of Ashford. His title derived from the Irish *Ard Oileáin*, a high island on the lake. It was said that he "treated his tenants kindly, had not pressed for rent, had advanced them *on credit* large quantities of meal during the winter of 1879-80, had clothed the poorest of them, and helped many to go to America as well as obtained some relief works for the valley."

But beyond the boundaries of Ardilaun's Eden, there was a growing tension. The murder of Lord Mountmorres in September 1880 and the boycotting of his widow brought home the unrest that was percolating throughout the countryside. In October 1880, Lord

Ardilaun and his agent received threatening letters, signed by "an Avenger," with a postmark of Birmingham. The writer warned His Lordship and agent that "a six-chamber revolver is ready for them on account of his tyrannical treatment of his mountain tenants." The *Times* of London found it necessary to remind its readers of Lord Ardilaun's generosity and that he had "expended £3,000 in providing meal for the people during their distress. They were profuse in their expressions of gratitude towards him."

Apparently, "expressions of gratitude" tapered off. Although many landlords requested police protection as a result of agrarian violence, not so Lord Ardilaun. Instead, he "organized a little bodyguard of his own people [usually his gamekeepers who were reported to be retired army] in preference to being followed about by the tall, dark figures now frequently seen everywhere in County Mayo." It became necessary to provide protection for Ardilaun's bailiffs as well. A reporter met "Ardilaun's agent walking, followed by two well-appointed constables with their rifles." And those rifles were not just for show. "A caretaker of Lord Ardilaun named Cartwright discovered last night two men taking away some timber from Rosshill, near Lough Mask. When they refused to bring it back, he fired at them wounding one severely."

On October 18, 1881, Charles Stewart Parnell and other Land League leaders imprisoned in Kilmainham Jail issued the "No Rent Manifesto." The manifesto called for "a campaign of passive resistance by the entire population of small tenant farmers by withholding rents [in order] to obtain large rent abatements under the second 1881 Irish Land Act." The aim of the manifesto was to draw attention to the inadequacy of the 1881 act in meeting core demands of the tenants, including the three "Fs" of fair rent, fixity of tenure, and free sale, as well as providing sufficient funds for occupier purchase. The purpose of the arrests of the leaders of the Land League was to cut the league off at its head. It was believed that this would cause a corresponding decrease in crime. Instead, crime greatly increased until such time as Parnell was released from jail in June.

In response to the manifesto, Ardilaun wrote a detailed letter to the *Times* of London in which he expressed his indignation at the refusal of his tenants to pay their rent. Prior to the emergence of the Land League, he had "lived among his people as much as he could [he was no absentee landlord], and he spent all the income of the property and more in improvements, in employing labour—insofar as they would allow him, in bettering the condition of the tenantry. As a natural consequence, he was much loved and honoured...and had much power and influence in the neighbourhood." But then the Land League came!

Ardilaun's response to Land League maneuvers was to join the Property Defence Association, an organization founded by members of the landed class in December 1880, soon after the murder of Lord Mountmorres. The association resisted boycotting and sent men to besieged estates so that landowners could sell livestock at auction and harvest crops. Another purpose was to secure English support for their organization and recognition of the dangers they faced in a disturbed Ireland. Ardilaun pointed out "the inequality of the struggle in Ireland, to murder and terrorism on one side, matched against the lawful modes of action, which alone are used on the other side, and asks: 'Will England look on while those loyal and true to her, and whom she is bound in honor and interest to protect, are overborn by American gold?'" "American gold" was a reference to the monetary support being funneled to Land League causes by Irish expatriates and their children.

Ardilaun's outburst shows a very narrow view of Irish history—one seen from the point of view of the landlord. "On the other side," to use his own words, is the weight of evidence showing that, for centuries, Irish tenants had borne the brunt of English policies—forced relocation, the Penal Laws, denial of the right to vote, the tithe tax, various coercion acts, packed juries—and that "justice" in Ireland rarely benefited the majority of Irishmen who were landless Catholics.

Earlier in 1881, Lord Ardilaun, in an attempt to prove his *bona fides* as a good landlord, had publicly exhibited his estate accounts from the time of his accession in 1868. The accounts listed expenditures for drainage and other improvements that cost one-third more per annum than the whole rental of his properties. But the accounts also showed that by far the largest expenditures were spent on compensation for disturbed tenants who had been removed to make way for Ashford House and its 200-acre park. In Lord Ardilaun's response to his critics, there is a tone deafness—a defect common among those to the manor born.

Despite his generosity, and the fact that over the course of a decade he had issued only ten ejectments for non-payment of rent, three years of poor harvests had left Ardilaun's tenants incapable of paying their rents. Events beyond his control and outside the boundaries of his castle-like oasis turned Ardilaun from benevolent landlord to oppressor in the eyes of his tenants.

With the Land League particularly active in Galway, an aroused peasantry was looking for a fight, and when Lord Ardilaun's agent instructed process server Joseph Huddy to deliver notice of ejectments to the tenants of Upper Cloughbrack in the heart of Joyce County, it got one.

JOYCE COUNTRY

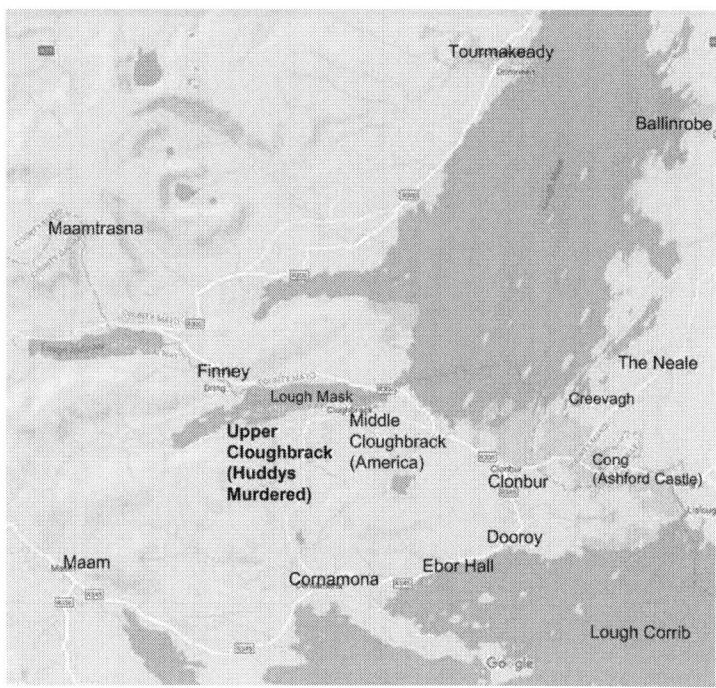

Ballinrobe – Market town and site of monster Land League rally
Clonbur – Patrick Kearney's public house where Mountmorres murder was plotted
Cong – Site of Ashford House, Home of Lord Ardilaun, and Cong Courthouse
Creevagh – Home of Joseph and John Huddy
Dooroy – Site of murder of Lord Mountmorres
Ebor Hall – Home of Lord Mountmorres
Finney – Site of police hut (Maamtrasna murders)
Maam – Site of hotel owned by Lord Leitrim as well as violent resistance to evictions
Maamtrasna – Site of the murder of the Joyce family
Middle Cloughbrack (America) – Home of Michael Flynn
Tourmakeady – Church where Tom Casey made his confession
Upper Cloughbrack – Site of the Huddy murders

Chapter 8
Murders of Joseph and John Huddy

Victims:
Joseph and John Huddy

Arrested:
Mathias Kerrigan
Patrick ("Patsy") Higgins (Long)
Patrick Higgins (Sarah)
Thomas Higgins
Michael Flynn
(A total of 17 men from Upper and Middle Cloughbrack were arrested.)

Informer:
Mathias Kerrigan

Police:
Inspector Owens
Major Bond
Sub-inspector James F. Gibbons

In Charge of Investigation:
Mr. Dennehy, R. M., A. Newton Brady, R. M., Richard C. Lynch
Mr. Burke, Mr. Lyster, R. M., Mr. Gardiner, R. M.
George Bolton, Crown Prosecutor

Process-server Joseph Huddy would have been familiar to the people of Upper Cloughbrack, a village on the southwest bank of an arm of Lough Mask. Irish poet and author Katherine Tynan, who knew

Huddy, described him as a man "who wore a Caroline hat, a brown frieze coat, and corduroy knickers with boxcloth leggings that ended in spats over his shoelaces. (An example of peasant attire is below.) The seventy-four-year old Joseph had lived for years in a cabin on the road between Ballinrobe and Hollymount, which was always under siege because of his occupation. He had been fired on [shot at] many times, once while attempting to break the blockade of Captain Boycott in 1880 and run supplies" to him.

Although a Kerry man from Southwest Ireland, Joseph Huddy had the reputation of being one of the most vicious process-servers in the West. Father Peter Waldron, a priest from Clonbur parish, denounced Joe from the pulpit as a cruel man, and in words that turned out to be prophetic, the reverend told his parishioners that, Joe "will never stop till he's put in a bag." Most congregants thought the priest meant that Joe would not cease his work as a process server until he was six feet under. Instead, it came very near to describing his fate at the hands of his killers. The harsh criticism was justified as Joe had earned his reputation. According to Katherine Tynan in her autobiographical *The Middle Years*:

> It was after the famine years that he made his name as a bailiff. [DeBurgh] D'Arcy of Houndswood was broke and his property sold in the Encumbered Estates Court. There were a lot of evictions on the estate and Joe was the bailiff. He was very good at the work; for when others of the Sheriff's posse held back Joe 'ud be up on the thatch of the wretched cabins with a crowbar, tearing the creatures' little homes to pieces [known as tumbling]. By this the people were prevented going back into the cabins, and had only the roadside, unless some charitable neighbour took them in.
>
> There was an eviction one day at a place called Townroe... The mothers...were thinking to stay there the night, as the lane was a No Man's Land. They had gathered sticks and lit a fire, and had hung a pot from a stick in the wall, and with a few handfuls of Indian meal they had, they were making stirabout. Joe came up with a great pretence of friendliness by the way that

he was going to light his pipe at the fire. He stood there, puffing at the pipe and talking quietly, till the stirabout was near cooked, and then, before anyone could hinder him, he pulled down a big stone from the top of the wall right into the pot, and the bottom was knocked out of the pot, and, all the poor hungry people's food spilled out on them. And with that he ran away.

On the morning of January 3, 1882, Joseph Huddy, who had served as bailiff for Lord Ardilaun and his father for more than three decades, as well as acting as a petty-sessions summons-server for the district, set out from his thirty-five-acre farm in Creevagh near Cong for the purpose of serving ejectment orders on tenants of Lord Ardilaun in the districts of Clonbur and Cornamona. Accompanying Joe was his seventeen-year-old grandson, John Huddy. Joseph Huddy, Jr. offered to go with his father to help serve the processes, "but the old man refused, saying that it would look as if he wanted protection."

On that winter's morning, Joe carried twelve processes for Upper Cloughbrack. He was to serve Mary Walsh, Bridgit Comer (Mary Walsh's mother), Patrick Moran, Michael Coyne, Stephen Coyne, Patrick Coyne, Luke Coyne, John Macken, Patrick Macken, Patrick Conroy, Patrick (Patsy) Higgins, and Mathias Kerrigan.

At the time, Upper Cloughbrack (Irish for speckled rock) was a densely populated area, consisting of small farms and wretched houses built closely together with no defined village center, the soil and vegetation fit only for the raising of sheep and the family cow. Each tenant held his house and garden separately, but sheep and cattle grazed in a common area in the more mountainous areas south of the village. Lord Ardilaun allowed his leaseholders to cut turf and hay for their own use but not for removal from the property; that is, the hay and turf could not be used as cash crops.[30]

The journey from Creevagh to Upper Cloughbrack would take the Huddys about an hour and a half, the car travelling west on a road paralleling Lough Mask and passing through the village of Middle

---

[30] According to Professor Pat Finnegan, "The period with most evictions extended from April 1881 to September 1882, with the peak occurring between January and June 1882," the time of the Ardilaun evictions. "The increase in evictions…probably indicates the desire of the landlords to rid themselves of 'bad' tenants before settlements under the Land Act of 1881 became widespread." *Loughrea*, p. 55.

Cloughbrack, also known as America because so many of its people had emigrated to the States. At 10:00 on that January morning, Joseph Huddy had Michael Coyne stop at a point in the road that led south to Cornamona as it would be necessary for the Huddys to continue from that point on foot, and Coyne was instructed to meet them in about an hour's time on the Cornamona Road. Before setting off through the fields to serve Mary Walsh, the elder Huddy told Coyne that the last process in his pocket was for Mathias Kerrigan.

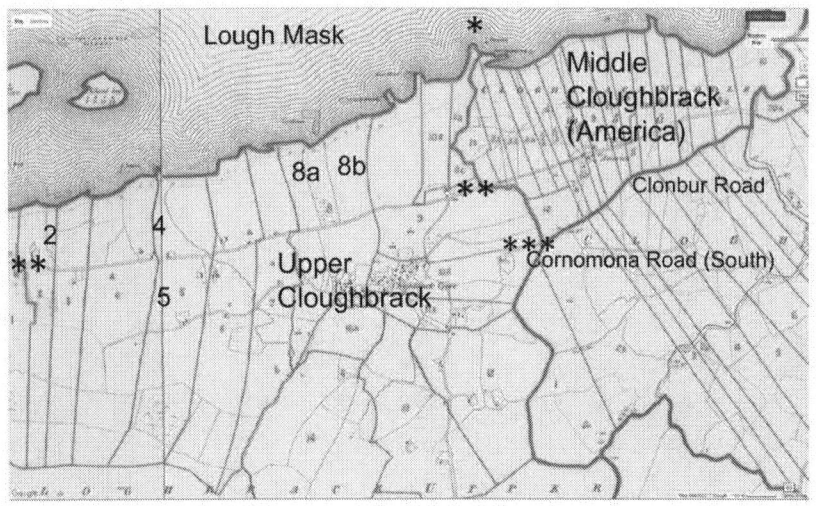

Lot 2, John "Luke" Holleran and son
Lot 4, Patrick Higgins (Long); Lot 5, Mathias Kerrigan
Lot 8a – Patrick Higgins (Sarah); Lot 8b, Patrick Mannion
*Site of boats
**Boreen
***Cornamona Road where driver Coyne waited for Huddys
(Approximate locations of lots based on Griffith's Valuation Survey of Galway completed in 1857)

After waiting for the Huddys' return at the assigned spot for several hours, at 4:00, with sunset approaching, Coyne drove on to Cornamona as the elder Huddy had told him that it was his intention to cross to an island in Lough Corrib where he was to serve additional processes. When Coyne reached Cornamona, he asked the police if they had seen the Huddys. They had not. At this time, the district was designated as being in a "disturbed state," and process servers were at a considerable risk of violence. Concerned about foul play, the police proceeded to Upper Cloughbrack to look for the missing Huddys. It was now dark, and the men were nowhere to be found. But enough evidence of a crime had been found at the house of Mathias Kerrigan to take Mathias and his fifteen-year-old son Matthew into custody.

The next day, the police returned and questioned all of the adults of Upper Cloughbrack, but no one had any information on the Huddys even though it was known from the driver that Huddy and his grandson had gone into Upper Cloughbrack for the purpose of serving ejectment papers the previous day. The police then questioned the children, but all they got out of the lads and lasses was: "Ni fhaca me Joe marbh na beo." ("I did not see Joe dead or alive.")

After tracing the Huddys' movements as far as the house of Mathias Kerrigan, the police made a thorough search of the property. During the search, they found evidence of a struggle in Kerrigan's yard as well as a mark made by a bullet in the wall of the gable end of Kerrigan's house and bloodstains on the wall.

Additional evidence was provided by two sons of Joseph Huddy, John and Thomas Huddy, who told the police that when their father and their nephew did not return home that evening, they went in search of them. Someone in the village sent them in the direction of Mathias Kerrigan's house and that was as far as the two missing men could be traced.[31]

> John Huddy swore to tracing the footprints of his father in a yard leading to Kerrigan's house. He knew them by the nails of the boot, which were of an unusual kind, and were specially put in his father's boots the day before for traveling purposes… He further testified that Kerrigan was engaged the day his father was missed in the barn threshing oats…
>
> Sub-inspector Smith proved that he was in charge of a party of police who went in search of the missing bailiffs, and found no tidings of them up till they came to Kerrigan's. They were

---

[31] At that time of year, sunset would have been around 4:30. However, on January 3, 1882, there was a full moon.

accompanied by Huddy's sons, who directed them. They found blood marks on the wall in various places, and also found that in some places, mud, etc., had been thrown or daubed across the blood marks in order to obliterate them. On one of the walls they found a bullet mark. They also found blood stains on some clothes of Kerrigan's.

Mr. H. A. Garde, agent to Lord Ardilaun, gave evidence, and said he had issued a writ two days before to the Kerrigans at the suit of Lord Ardilaun, which Huddy had in his possession. Kerrigan…repeatedly denied that any blood stains were found in his house or on his clothes, and denied all knowledge of the deed.

Resident Magistrate Dennehy and Constabulary Inspector Owens initiated a far-ranging search for the bodies of the Huddys. Sixty police were detailed for the investigation. For four days, the police dug up bogland and searched the mountains without result. According to the *Dublin Daily Express*:

> The people in the district are chiefly an Irish-speaking population, and they did not at all seem disposed to give any information. On Saturday, Mr. Smyth obtained the services of two bloodhounds from Ashford House, but no clue of the whereabouts of the missing men could be obtained. It then became the general impression that the bodies were conveyed to the lake and thrown in.

At this time, a navigable waterway existed between Lough Corrib and Galway Bay by way of the Corrib River at Cong. The services of Her Majesty's Royal Navy were engaged, and forty men of HMS *Banterer*, then lying in Galway Bay, were sent to Cong. At one point, it became necessary for the seamen to carry a pinnace, a light boat propelled by oars or sails, a distance of seven miles from Cong to Lough Mask. Their search of the lake was described as "unremitting."

For twelve days, the "bluejackets harrowed and dragged the bottom of the lake, their efforts frequently hampered by rough waters." Then on Friday, January 27th, they concentrated their efforts in a particular spot. It was rumored that information as to where the bodies could be found had been provided by an old woman who had seen a number of men row out onto the lake and drop two large, heavy bags into the water. The *Guardian* reported that:

> A grappling iron caught upon something weighty, which on being brought to the surface proved to be the body of the younger of the two missing men. The body was tied up in a sack in to which he had been put head foremost.... The sack was too short to contain the entire body, and the mouth of it was firmly tied with a hair rope around the legs of the deceased a little above the knees. The body was in a wonderful state of preservation. It was removed to a small island hard by, and the men returned to resume the work of dredging for the second body. This was found about twenty minutes later, only a few yards from the spot where the first body had been found. The murderers had not taken the trouble to put the old man's body in a sack. They merely wrapped his own overcoat around him, and having firmly fastened a large stone round his legs, threw him into the water... The old man's body was also very little decomposed.[32]

A Ballinrobe correspondent for the *Guardian* reported on what occurred after the bodies were recovered:

> It was not without some difficulty that the bodies were lifted into the boat, a quantity of stones having been placed in the sacks, and a stone weighing about three-quarters of a hundredweight having been suspended by a rope from the neck of the young man. Captain Morant, who was in charge of the *Banterer*, had the bodies at once tied up together in a sail-cloth, and forwarded to the shore, where a party of ten constables, in charge of Major Bond, R. M., awaited them and removed them to a temporary police barrack. A few minutes later the bodies were placed on an outside jaunting car, and the remains were conveyed to the Clonbur courthouse [described in the *Irish Times* as a "wretched building"]. Shortly after the bodies had been

---

[32] During the trials, Police Constable Dowd testified that a huge stone, "as heavy as one man could conveniently carry," had been placed in the basket with the elder Huddy. In court, a "huge stone" was produced—the stone that had been placed in the sack with the young John Huddy.

there deposited, the female friends of the deceased were admitted, and a sad scene of grief and distress followed.

After the bodies were recovered, a paralysis caused by fear gripped the district. At an appearance before the compensation board in December 1882, Mr. MacDermott, Q. C. stated that "As an instance of the feeling existing in the locality, counsel remarked on the behavior of the coroner's jury who were sworn at the inquest and who absolutely refused, on pain of being locked up for the night, to say that the Huddys had been feloniously killed."

When questioned, Michael Coyne, the driver of the jaunting car, told the police that he did not hear any shots fired. However, other villagers stated that they *did* hear shots between twelve and one o'clock.

The police, now believing that the death of the Huddys was the result of an entire village rising up against the process servers, arrested, in addition to Mathias Kerrigan and his son, fifteen men on suspicion of complicity in the murders.[33]

On January 31st, nearly four weeks after they had been arrested, the suspects appeared before Mr. Dennehy, R. M., Mr. Burke, and Mr. Richard C. Lynch in Clonbur, having traveled by steamer from Galway City Jail to Cong. After their arrival in Cong, the men were transported to Clonbur on cars under a strong police escort and were remanded for a week. On February 7th, the seventeen men again appeared before the magistrates. Five were released and twelve remanded. "The Crown Solicitor based his application for a remand...on the difficulties arising from the reticence of the people with regard to the crime... Such terrorism existed so that everybody who came forward to give information did so with his life in his hands, and until this state of things was in some degree abated, witnesses would not be inclined to present themselves."

---

[33] According to the *Freeman's Journal*, the twelve men were: Luke Kerrigan, John Kerrigan (Bolrawn), Martin Kerrigan, Patrick Kerrigan (Mark), Michael Coyne (the driver), Patrick Higgins, Michael Flynn, Michael Higgins, Thomas Flynn, Patrick Kerrigan, John Kerrigan, Thomas Higgins, John "Luke" Holleran, John Kerrigan, and Michael Mulroe. These arrests were made on two subsequent nights when most people would have been in their cottages. ("The Lough Mask Tragedy," February 8, 1882) It would appear to be a sweep of anyone named Kerrigan.

The Crown Solicitor was right to question the reticence of the people of Upper Cloughbrack. Although these murders had taken place in broad daylight, little information had been gleaned from repeated interviews with the villagers. In an editorial dated December 11, 1882, before the start of the second trial of Patrick Higgins, the editor of the *Times* of London wrote: "For months the fate [of the Huddys] was a mystery, until at length their bodies were found sunk in Lough Mask. During all that time scores of people must have known the truth and talked of it among themselves. They made no sign and uttered no word. The terror of the organization [the land League] which executed its judgment upon the old man Huddy and his grandson sealed the lips even of the innocent spectators of a premeditated butchery, in which by a fiendish craft as many persons as possible were forced to take some indirect part... We are presented with the spectacle of a crime organized and premeditated and carried into effect with the complicity of the whole country-side."

Despite the frustrations of the *Times* editor, in the recent past, a collective silence had achieved the desired results. The killers of Lord Leitrim and Lord Mountmorres never went to trial, and agrarian agitators, who had committed numerous outrages throughout the West, had gotten away with their crimes. However, there *was* a difference for those accused of the Huddy killers. The provisions of The Coercion Act of January 1881 gave the Crown expanded powers to hold suspects. After multiple remands, it is likely that Kerrigan believed that the Crown could hold him indefinitely—a misconception that the Government was unlikely to refute.

The twelve men held on remand were back in front of the magistrates on February 14th. At that hearing, the Crown Solicitor asked for another remand. Although reluctantly given, the prosecution's request was granted, but the magistrates insisted that at the next appearance evidence would have to be brought forward or the men would be released.

On February 21st, six weeks after they had been arrested, the twelve men again stood before the magistrates, at which time, the prosecuting solicitor said that he "did not deem it expedient to proceed with the charge, but intimated that the accused might hereafter be again called up. The men were then discharged by the magistrates but were immediately re-arrested under The Protection Act as principals in the murder." Eventually, all were released—all except Mathias Kerrigan.

That summer, Mathias Kerrigan was imprisoned in a damp jail cell, measuring 16 feet by 5-1/2 feet, in Galway City. A straw mattress, two sheets, each marked "Galway Gaol," two blankets, and a quilt were provided by his jailers. Exercise in the yard was conducted in single file; conversation was prohibited.[34]

As Kerrigan languished, the Crown's case seemed to stall.[35] But that was about to change. In August, the investigation was turned over to George Bolton, Crown Prosecutor for Tipperary. Along with Bolton, a team of investigators and police, fanned out across the district with the full weight of the law behind them. In the end, 211 witnesses were questioned under Bolton's supervision.

George Bolton, a tall, thin, bald man, with a long white beard and cold black eyes, was a force to be reckoned with. His approach to questioning witnesses was to "confound them, cow them, confuse them into making statements." Father Jarlath Waldron, author and local historian, described Bolton's technique in examining witnesses in his book *Maamtrasna, The Murders and the Mystery*:

> Always accompanied by eight or more of the tallest, beefiest RIC [Royal Irish Constabulary] men he could select, he would stalk into the cabin of a suspect, eject everybody, commandeer a chair (if there were such), on which he would sit in majestic state, the representative of the Queen… One by one he would interview the household, beginning with the youngest. His very presence was forbidding and frightening. His silences were menacing, but when he spoke, he spoke with a shattering voice… Whether innocent or guilty of any misdemeanors, they trembled like trees before a gale.

---

[34] Under The Coercion Act, "Those detained were not treated as convicts. Their families were eligible for outdoor relief at a rate of £1 per week, and their continued detention was reviewed every three months." Finnegan, *Loughrea.*, p. 83.

[35] It is possible that the reason for the inaction during the summer of 1882 was that in August, the police were fully focused on the mass murder of the John Joyce family at Maamtrasna in the Maamtrasna Mountains in Galway.

One man had reason to tremble. On September 19, 1882, when Mathias Kerrigan appeared before Magistrate Brady, with the Crown represented by George Bolton, he was charged with "participation" in the Huddy murders. No solicitor appeared for the defense, and the witness was questioned in private.

On September 24th, fifteen residents were interviewed by the police in Clonbur, and the first cracks in the dam appeared. James Burke deposed that he had heard several shots coming from the Kerrigans' yard. John "Luke" Holleran and his son also reported hearing shots from the Kerrigan yard as well as seeing Patrick Higgins in the boreen. Tom Mannion, Patrick's son, a man of about thirty-two years, stated that when he saw Tom Higgins coming down the lane, Higgins had told him that he had better get off the boreen. Several women, who had previously denied that the Huddys had even been in Upper Cloughbrack, admitted that they had seen the Huddys walking in the direction of the Kerrigan house.

Among those questioned on September 24th were Kate Higgins, daughter of Patrick Higgins (Long), and Mary Conroy, a cousin of Kate Higgins. Their testimony, which would change radically from the time they were interviewed in their homes and in Clonbur by Brady and Bolton and their appearance in a Dublin courtroom, would prove fatal to Patrick Higgins's defense.

On September 25th, only one person was called before Resident Magistrate A. Newton Brady for questioning. The *Freeman's Journal* reported that Mary Kerrigan, Mathias's twenty-three-year-old daughter, had been interviewed in Clonbur. In that interview, Mary stated that she had seen the bailiffs going in the direction of her father's house—a remarkable admission from Kerrigan's own daughter—but one that shines a light on the intensity of the interviews.

On September 26th, Kerrigan was "fully committed to trial." According to Bolton, in an account he wrote of cases he had prosecuted in the early 1880s, Kerrigan "began to fear the evidence we [the Crown] had procured might possibly place himself in a dangerous position; and, after having kept the secret for over eight months, he gave me a full statement of the occurrence. This enabled us to procure the evidence of other witnesses, who, when they found we were in possession of the facts, were afraid not to tell what they knew." Among those who were convinced to cooperate were John "Luke" Holleran, Holleran's son John, and a man named Michael Moran.

After turning "approver," the term used for an informer, Mathias Kerrigan provided Bolton with the names of the three men whom he claimed were responsible for the murders of Joseph and John Huddy: Thomas Higgins, Patrick Higgins (Long), and Michael Flynn. The head constable traveled the forty miles to Upper and Middle Cloughbrack and arrested and charged with murder the persons named by Kerrigan. Also arrested was Patrick Higgins (Sarah) who was charged with being an accessory to murder. At that time, Kerrigan was released from custody.

With the establishment of the Dublin Commission, legislated under the terms of The Crimes Act, judges now tried agrarian murders and outrages before special juries in venues other than the home county. One of those trials was that of Patrick Walsh, the accused killer of John Lydon and his son Martin in Letterfrack, Galway in May 1881. Lydon had been killed after taking over a farm from which another had been evicted. The trial had been moved from Galway to Dublin as it was believed that jurors were "so demoralized by fear owing to the recent outrages and the general state of intimidation which prevails…that no one man on such a jury dare propose to find him guilty and that there is a certainty of acquittal." The Government's intended goal of facilitating a conviction by a change of venue had succeeded. Walsh was found guilty and hanged in Galway Jail in September 1882.

Upon application by Crown counsel, Queen's Bench, Dublin, an order was executed, transferring from Galway to Dublin the trials of Patrick Higgins, Thomas Higgins, and Michael Flynn for the murders of the two Huddys. The *Morning News* of Belfast wrote that "Kerrigan and his family have left Galway for Dublin. The police are in charge of Kerrigan's house."

This change of venue proved devastating to the defense of these rural Irish-Catholic defendants. In Dublin, the jury would be composed of English-speaking Protestant shopkeepers sympathetic to the Crown, especially in light of the assassination of Frederick Cavendish, the newly appointed Chief Secretary for Ireland, and William Burke, Permanent Under-secretary, in the spring of 1882 in Phoenix Park, Dublin. With the assassination of two representatives of the Her Majesty, the possibility existed that the jury would be predisposed to convict people accused of violent crimes. Additionally, the defendants lacked an understanding of the judicial system and were prevented by law from testifying on their own behalf. Their native tongue was Irish, and it would be necessary to rely on an interpreter throughout the proceedings to convey their words to the judge and jury. Constable Thomas Evans, the interpreter, "spoke Ulster Irish and was not familiar with the Connaught Irish spoken by the defendants."[36] As the three men travelled to Dublin, they must have been seized by a sense of doom.

Each man was to be tried individually, and their cases were brought before a grand jury in Dublin on December 6, 1882, with Justice William O'Brien presiding. After paying homage to Lord Ardilaun, who was in the courtroom, the judge addressed the men of the jury in regard to the Lough Mask murders: "I apprehend from my perusal of the depositions which have been made in this case, that you will have no difficulty whatsoever in performing the duty asked of you by law… If you take the witnesses of the name of Kerrigan, all members of the same family, and a witness named Mannion…, they all depose to the fact of this crime apparently in terms sufficiently distinct and explicit to warrant you in finding a bill for murder." The grand jury obliged, and true bills were returned.

---

[36] "Maamtrasna: The Trial of Myles Joyce in 1882," Niamh Howlin, University of Dublin Sutherland School of Law, 2017.

Chapter 9
Maamtrasna Massacre and Phoenix Park Murders

Between the time of the murders of Joseph and John Huddy and the trials of the three men accused of their murders, two events took place in Ireland that had a profound effect on the outcome of their trials.

During the summer of 1882, while the villagers of Middle and Upper Cloughbrack continued to maintain a collective silence about the murders of Joseph and John Huddy, a horrific scene of violence was being investigated in the village of Maamtrasna, an enclave in the mountains of Maamtrasna overlooking, from a distance, Lough Mask and Lough Nafooey (the Lake of Hatred). But before the Maamtrasna Massacre in August, another horrible event occurred in May. The new Chief Secretary to the Lord Lieutenant of Ireland and Permanent Under-secretary were attacked with knives by members of the Invincibles, a splinter group of the Irish Republican Brotherhood, in Phoenix Park, Dublin. The brutality of their deaths appalled even those who had become desensitized to the violence in Ireland.

Lord Frederick Cavendish was born in 1836, the second son of the 7th Duke of Devonshire and husband to a favorite niece of Prime Minister Gladstone. Gladstone vigorously advanced his nephew-in-law's career through Britain's political landscape. In 1872, during the prime minister's first administration, Cavendish became private secretary to Gladstone. He went on to serve as Lord of the Treasury and Financial Secretary to the Treasury.

In May 1882, William E. Forster resigned as Chief Secretary to the Lord Lieutenant in protest of the Kilmainham Treaty and the release from prison of Charles Stewart Parnell and his compatriots. While imprisoned in Kilmainham Jail, Parnell had engaged in a series of negotiations with Gladstone's Government with Captain William O'Shea acting as his intermediary.[37] In return for a promise from Parnell to use his position as the leader of the Land League to quell the violence in Ireland, the Government agreed to settle the "rent arrears" question that would allow 100,000 tenants to appeal for fair rent before the land courts. This was regarded as a major victory for the land-reform movement.

Forster's resignation left open one of the most thankless jobs in British Government. When Gladstone appointed Frederick Cavendish as Chief Secretary, it was met with derision as Cavendish had a speech impediment—a definite handicap for a representative of Her Majesty's Government in Ireland. Even so, he was considered competent—and he *was* married to Gladstone's niece—and so off to Ireland he went.

Cavendish arrived in Ireland on May 6, 1882 and immediately went to Dublin Castle where he took the oath of office and introduced himself to the staff. From there, he was to go to the Chief Secretary's Lodge in Phoenix Park. As he walked along Chesterfield Avenue, a cab, carrying Permanent Under-secretary Thomas Burke, the most senior Irish civil servant, got out and joined him. As they neared the Viceregal Lodge, Burke was set upon by five or six members of the Invincibles. When Cavendish attempted to assist Burke, another assailant attacked him with a knife. Both men died at the scene

The Invincibles, a heretofore unknown group, introduced itself to Ireland by leaving cards with all the major newspapers, claiming responsibility for the deaths of Cavendish and Burke.

It was Burke, not Cavendish, who had been the target of the Invincibles. The group had planned to kill Burke the previous day but had missed him in the park. Unfortunately, for Cavendish, a second attempt on the Permanent Under-secretary was scheduled for the day of Cavendish's arrival in Ireland. The Invincibles had chosen Burke as its target because it was he who had been responsible for executing Forster's policies under The Coercion Act. Under the act, more than

---

[37] Katherine "Kitty" O'Shea, wife of Captain William O'Shea, maintained a long-term relationship with Charles Stewart Parnell that produced three children. O'Shea knew about his wife's infidelity but did not object. (He had his own mistress.) But when O'Shea was denied an inheritance from Kate's aunt, he filed for divorce, exposing the adulterous relationship and Parnell to charges of immorality.

nine hundred members of the Land League had been arrested, including Charles Stewart Parnell. It is possible that if Forster had not resigned, it would have been Forster, and not Cavendish, who would have been murdered by the Invincibles on that spring day.[38]

In the wake of the Phoenix Park assassinations, The Coercion Act was again introduced in Ireland. Section 16 of the act allowed for a Star Chamber inquiry, that is, the right of the state to summon a suspect for interrogation under oath and *without legal representation*. Each witness could be compelled to give evidence in any subsequent trial, and if they refused, faced imprisonment. When George Bolton took over the Huddy murder investigation in September 1882, Section 16 compelled all those designated as witnesses to appear in Dublin at the trial of the accused.

The second event was not political, but tribal. Even so, it had an impact on the trials of Patrick Higgins, Thomas Higgins, and Michael Flynn.

Early on the morning of August 18, 1882, Maamtrasna native John Collins walked to the house of neighbor John Joyce to borrow a pair of wool cards. As he approached the cottage, Collins noticed that the door was off its hinges, and when he entered the house, he saw, lying on the floor, John Joyce, lifeless and naked.

After alerting the villagers to his discovery, Collins and several others returned to the house where they found, in addition to John Joyce's body, the bodies of Bridgit "Breege" Joyce, the wife of John Joyce; John's aged mother, Margaret; and Peggy, John's daughter from his first marriage. The three women had been beaten to a pulp. In the house with the four bodies were Joyce's two sons, Michael, about seventeen, and Patrick "Patsy" Joyce, a lad of about eleven years. Both boys had been savagely attacked. Michael, who had been shot in the head and stomach, was near death and would die later that day.

---

[38] Five men, Joseph Brady, Daniel Curley, Michael Fagan, Thomas Caffrey, and Timothy Kelly, were executed in Dublin in May and June 1883 for their roles in the murders of Cavendish and Burke. Several others received sentence of penal servitude for their part in the plot. Informer James Carey was fatally shot at sea by Patrick O'Donnell on the *Melrose* on his way to South Africa with his family. O'Donnell was hanged in England for Carey's murder although he claimed he had fired his pistol in self-defense after Carey had drawn a weapon.

After much discussion, some villagers went to the temporary police hut at Finney, two miles from the murder scene, where they told Constable Johnston of the massacre. Along with Sub-constable Lenihan, Johnston followed the villagers to the scene. He found Michael Joyce lying in bed very near to death:

> I asked Michael, through Sub-constable Lenihan who spoke Irish, what had happened to them last night? Michael Joyce said in reply that the two or three men came into the room and shot him in bed and that he saw one of the men take up something like a stick and strike his sister and that he heard his grandmother screaming. About the break of day, he said, he got out of bed and came down to the kitchen for a drink and said he saw his father lying on the kitchen floor. After getting the drink, he returned to the bed in the kitchen where his stepmother was lying. She was then living. Before the men came into the room, he heard shots. I asked Michael how many men did he see and if he knew them? He said no, that *their faces were blackened* and that there were three or four men. I then asked Pat Joyce…did he know them and he said no, that their *faces were blackened*. I asked if they had a light, he said yes, a piece of bogdeal. I found a bullet on the floor near where John Joyce was lying.[39]

John Joyce was described as "a small farmer holding six pounds worth of land. His house was a hovel, his land, a patch of potatoes and cabbage… He had the grazing of a mountainside, whereon his cows fed free. There was nothing in the shape of furniture in the house… No window threw light into the domicile. A hole in the wall of the second chamber (about one square foot) gave all the ventilation and illumination it possessed and the fire was simply made by burning peat on the floor." Lord Spencer, who visited the site a month after the murders, declared that the Joyce house would not be used for pigs in England.

The savagery of the attacks was unlike anything the police had ever witnessed. Although the Government was quick to blame the deaths

---

[39] The testimony of these two boys—that their assailants had "blackened faces"—would be deliberately kept from defense counsel as well as the juries at the trials of the eight men charged with the Joyce murders, resulting in a fatal miscarriage of justice for Myles Joyce and the imprisonment of four innocent men.

on agrarian violence, the crime didn't fit the model. If Joyce and his family were being punished by organized agitators, what had been their crime?

A theory arose that Margaret Joyce, John's mother, had told the police that on a visit to Upper Cloughbrack, she had seen where the bodies of Joseph and John Huddy had been dumped into Lough Mask. But the tale doesn't bear scrutiny. Supposedly, Margaret Joyce was visiting her son (a man named O'Brien) in the village at the time of the Huddy murders. Would a visitor, and one of such an advanced age, jump into the middle of that mess, possibly endangering her son by her betrayal? Other questions arose: Why would it have taken seven months for members of a secret society to take revenge for the betrayal of the three men accused of the Huddy murders? And why kill the whole family for the sin of the mother? At the time of the Joyce murders, no one in Upper Cloughbrack had been charged with the murders of the Huddys. The case was solved only after Mathias Kerrigan turned informer in late September, a month after the Joyce family was annihilated.

Another story that gained traction was that Peggy Joyce, a pretty girl of seventeen, was the real cause for the slaughter. A police hut, supervised by Constable Johnston, had been erected near the Joyce home. Assigned to this hut were four sub-constables who regularly patrolled the mountainous area around Maamtrasna (probably looking for stills to make poteen). It was said that Peggy had engaged in a flirtation with these constables, and the young men had found excuses to visit the Joyce home, their comings and goings observed by the villagers. It was also said that during these visits, information had been provided to the police by the Joyce family. But if the purpose of these visits was for police to gain information, their efforts had failed. There were no arrests of agitators, no actionable intelligence gained.

The only reason to tie the Huddy and Joyce murders together was to promote the Government's entrenched belief that all violence was now agrarian and could be placed at the door of the Land League. But the Joyce murders gave every appearance of being caused by bad blood—more Hatfields and McCoys than the work of a secret society using violence as a means to an end.

A possible motive for the murders was explored by Father Jarlath Waldron in his exhaustive account of the Joyce murders, *Maamtrasna,*

The Murders and the Mystery. Father Waldron, a local historian, believes that the murders of the Joyces was not in reprisal for some unknown act of betrayal but, rather, a death sentence for the more mundane crime of sheep-stealing.

> John Joyce was unquestionably the champion sheep-stealer in the Valley. In fact, he was a kleptomaniac. Anything from a goose to a piece of homespun—anything he clapped his eyes on—could finish up in his house before nightfall. A tall man of prodigious strength, he was a renowned fighting man in an age when such ability was valued... He was rarely satisfied with just one [pig]. He was seen one morning—well after sun-up—calmly driving home no less than five fine hoggets which he had just stolen from Big John Casey of Bunachrick... There was a bitter personal spleen between these two men.

Father Waldron suggested a second motive for the killings: personal vendetta. "There is a local tradition of a meeting held, prior to the murder, at which one hundred people were alleged to have been present—to settle, once and for all, the frustrations caused by John Joyce and his like. As the murder party set out, allegedly under the influence of alcohol, on a wild and crazy vendetta...rumours of the family of John Joyce becoming informers could have been the final straw to break the patience of frustrated neighbors."

The men chosen to investigate the Maamtrasna murders were Resident Magistrate A. Newton Brady and Crown Prosecutor for Tipperary George Bolton. After Bolton and his men had done their work, ten men from the area were arrested and charged with murder, but the investigation and trials were farces as the evidence presented by the Crown was a pack of lies.

In an act of revenge, three members of another Joyce family from Bunachrick, a nearby village, had made up a story entirely out of whole cloth about witnessing the actual murders. In their tale, they tracked the supposed killers a great distance, in the dark, with one of them barefoot—an assertion ridiculous on its face as you cannot go ten feet in that terrain without the risk of falling in a hole or tripping over a rock. Discrepancies, contradictions, varying number of killers, and a house facing in the wrong direction—none of it mattered. In fact, "Judge Barry, in his charge to the jury, said that the discrepancy as to the number of participants in the murders was proof of the truth of the statements the informers had made." It didn't make sense then, and it doesn't make sense now. Of the ten men named by the fabricating Joyces, only three were actually guilty of the crime, and their participation in the murders had been a matter of guesswork on the part of their accusers.

After the conviction of the first three men tried for the murders, two of the accused, who had nothing to do with the killings, turned informers and gave the police the names of the men fed to them by Crown Prosecutor George Bolton during their interrogations. In order to save their lives, four of the accused, who had yet to go to trial, confessed to a crime they did not commit on the advice of their priest, Father Michael McHugh of Clonbur, who believed that "such a huge wrong could not continue [and] saw a probability of these men coming back to their wives and families and homes without a stain on their character." Unfortunately, this was Ireland, and the accused were Irish Catholics, and so the results were quite different from what Father McHugh had intended.

Father McHugh was criticized for his intervention, but Member of Parliament Tim Harrington came to his defense as well as the defense of the men who confessed to murders they did not commit: "It may be well for persons of noble sentiment and high mental culture to state they would face a murderer's death rather than admit a murder they never committed, but these men are ignorant, poverty-stricken, wretched peasants to whom the choice between immediate, ignominious death and confinement with the hope of release and vindication made all the difference in the world."

Two of the three men sentenced to death, Patrick Joyce and Patrick Casey, were guilty of the murders, and shortly before their executions, admitted their guilt and exonerated the third man, Myles Joyce of Cappanacreha. Pleas for a commutation of Myles's sentence fell on the deaf ears of Earl Spencer, Lord Lieutenant of Ireland, stating that "the law must take its course." Those who had made the false accusations went unpunished and spent the remainder of their days in Maamtrasna. But there were consequences, at least for their leader, John Casey of Bunachrick. Knowing of Casey's guilt, the parish priest denied him access to the confessional until he admitted his role in the murders—something Big John Casey never did.

Why had this terrible miscarriage of justice happened? According to Father Waldron, "Lives had been taken and…innocent people had suffered because a few of themselves saw in this murder a heaven-sent opportunity to be rid of some troublesome neighbors. Almost certainly, the three Joyce independent witnesses had never anticipated such an ending…[but] the three Joyces did not count on being confronted by a ruthless sharpie like Bolton."

In his determination to secure convictions, George Bolton had deliberately suppressed evidence—that of the men having darkened faces, making identification impossible—and keeping important information from the attorneys defending the innocent men—evidence that would have crippled the Crown's case. Much of this was revealed years later by Timothy Harrington, M. P., in his statements to the Parnell Commission, but it was too late for Myles Joyce, who protested his innocence with the last bit of breath in him: "I will see Jesus Christ in a short while—he too was unjustly hanged… I am going… God help my wife and her five orphans." To this day, there are those who are asking Her Majesty's Government to address an ancient wrong by exonerating Myles Joyce. But it is likely that Myles Joyce's name will never be cleared. Then, as now, it is not in the interest of the Government to acknowledge that an innocent man was executed. (See Chapter 16 and Appendix A for more information on the Maamtrasna Massacre as well as a 2017 paper by Niamh Howlin, University of Dublin Sutherland School of Law, "Maamtrasna: The Trial of Myles Joyce in 1882.")

The importance of the Maamtrasna murders and the Phoenix Park assassinations is that it seemed to confirm to the authorities in Dublin and London that Ireland had become ungovernable, and was there greater proof than that of the slaying of five souls in a remote mountain village and the assassination of representatives of Her Majesty in a public park in Dublin? Civilized people were tired of all of the violence and bloodshed, many of whom would soon sit on the juries that would decide if the three men accused of the Huddy murders would live or die.

The Huddy Murder Trials

Charged:
Patrick (Patsy) Higgins (Long) – Murder
Thomas Higgins – Murder
Michael Flynn – Murder
Patrick Higgins (Sarah) – Accessory

Witnesses:
Kate Higgins, daughter of defendant Patrick Higgins (Long)
Mary Conroy, friend of Kate Higgins
Judy Higgins Holleran, sister of Thomas Higgins
Sally Laffy, friend of Judy Higgins Holleran
Mathias Kerrigan
Bridgit Kerrigan, Wife of Mathias Kerrigan
Matthew and Martin Kerrigan, Sons of Mathias Kerrigan
Patrick and Tom Mannion
John "Luke" Holleran and son John

Judge:
Justice William O'Brien

Prosecution:
George Bolton, Chief Crown Prosecutor
M. P., Mr. James Murphy, Q. C.
Mr. Peter "Packer" O'Brien, Q. C.
Solicitor General A. M. Porter (Thomas and Patrick Higgins)
Solicitor General McCaffery (Michael Flynn)

Defense:
C. H. Teeling and Richard Adams
Instructed by P. J. Daly of Ballinrobe, County Mayo

Chapter 10
First Trial
of Patrick Higgins

Green Street Courthouse, Dublin with Raised Table and Witness Chair

After several delays, most involving subpoenas issued to witnesses for the defense and arrangements for travel from Galway to Dublin, the trial of Patrick Higgins (Long) commenced on December 7, 1882. Higgins had been brought to the Green Street Courthouse, Dublin, from Kilmainham Jail with a "strong police escort." Higgins, who was about sixty years old and over the middle height [maybe 5'-9"], was dressed in a "shabby, threadbare suit of grey frieze, and his coat is of the swallow-tail make, in fashion amongst the older generations of the Irish peasantry. He wore about his neck a red woolen muffler. His hair is grey and very long, and he has a long black beard. Like all the other men recently tried for agrarian crimes, he wears a moustache, an ornament until lately foreign to the fashions of the peasantry." Higgins pleaded not guilty to the charges.

A dozen Royal Marines, who had been deputized as policemen, guarded the court. Present in the courtroom were Lord Ardilaun, employer of Joseph Huddy, and Colonel Jenkinson, the head of the Criminal Investigation Department. On that first day, it was standing room only. The accused, who spoke only Irish, and who was described by Justice O'Brien as "an almost dumb and silent spectator of a scene in which his life and death were involved," required an interpreter throughout the proceedings. Head Constable Evans, who had translated for the accused in the Maamtrasna murders the previous month, was again sworn.

A critique of the interpreter can be found in the transcript of the Parnell Commission of September 1888. It would be laughable, except that three lives depended on the accuracy of Head Constable Evans's words:

> The interpreter, speaking in a hard, rapid, clattering voice, was almost as unintelligible as the Erse-speaking witness. The Bench could not hear him. Counsel could not hear him. To make himself heard, the interpreter moved off to the extremity of the solicitor's bench. Then it was found that he was too far away from his witness. They craned their necks, each in the other's direction, the interpreter turning his hand into an ear-trumpet, the witness doing likewise, as they bawled in their diverse tongues. Kerrigan was the Erse witness's name; and Kerrigan almost howled when he told the Court that he had been nine months in jail on suspicion of having murdered the two Huddys.

Irish author, Katharine Tynan, was also present at the Huddy trials:

> Quite by accident, I was put to wait till a seat in the court was found for me, into the room with the relatives of the men who were being tried for the murder. They were all women-folk, and I can remember to this day the strange pathos of the hooded figures, some of them nursing a baby at the breast, seated on the wooden benches around the walls. They were like so many Fates, these creatures of a destiny too strong for them, helpless, uncomplaining, doomed. Afterwards I saw the trial of the Irish-

speaking peasants for the murder. The evidence had all to be translated by an interpreter. I remember how they protested their innocence, their arms extended in the shape of a cross, murmuring their deep Irish, their tragic, haggard faces uplifted to the judge who was to condemn them.

The Crown was represented by Solicitor General A. M. Porter, M. P., Mr. James Murphy, Q. C., and Mr. Peter O'Brien, Q. C. and instructed by Mr. George Bolton, Special Crown Prosecutor. Appearing for the defense were Mr. C. H. Teeling and Mr. Richard Adams and instructed by Mr. P. J. Daly of Ballinrobe.

A wood-framed plaster model had been built showing the house where the men had been murdered, the surrounding fields, a boreen (a rugged lane usually too narrow for a jaunting car) that ran the length of the western part of the village, dividing the properties of Patrick Higgins and Mathias Kerrigan. The model was used to trace the movements of the two Huddys.

The process server's first stop was at the home of Mary Comer Walsh, who was still in bed when Huddy knocked on her door. She testified that a boy was with the elder Huddy and that she was served with a notice of ejectment.[40] The Huddys then cut across the fields and stopped at the house of Pat Moran, and the ejectment decree was served on his wife Catherine as Pat was away at the funeral of Joe Joyce. After passing the homes of Patrick Coyne and another named Kenny, in America (Middle Cloughbrack), they were seen walking along the main road. They then passed homes tenanted by James Flynn and another by John Macken, also of Middle Cloughbrack. At that hour of the morning, many people were still eating their breakfast, but witnesses swore that the Huddys were alive when they passed the house of James Flynn. The trace was lost at the corner of the boreen.

William Henry Good, an employee of Burke and Darley, land agents to Lord Ardilaun, testified that on December 1, 1881 he had given Joseph Huddy several ejectment processes, one of which was to

---

[40] At the trial of Thomas Higgins, an annoyed Mary Walsh stated that she had "sworn the truth twenty times," an indicator of the constant police presence in Upper Cloughbrack as well as George Bolton's persistent interrogators. She testified that Joe Huddy had awoken her in order to serve her the decree. After being served, she went back to bed.

be served on Patrick Higgins, the accused, who owed Lord Ardilaun three and a half years rent or about £5, 10s. Mr. Good explained that in serving ejectment processes, the bailiff served the tenant in default with a copy of the decree, keeping the original for his records. Mr. Good testified that he never saw the documents again, inferring that Patrick Higgins had, in fact, been served as both the original and copy were missing.

Evidence was then introduced regarding the discovery of the bodies in Lough Mask. "Both men were found…to have been assassinated by pistol and gunshot wounds. One of them [the boy] was found tied up in a sack, both of them had weights attached, stones, to keep them from rising."[41]

The next witness was Mathias Kerrigan, about fifty years of age, a tenant of Lord Ardilaun.[42] Kerrigan, who had turned informer after being detained without charge for nine months, stated that he had learned from his wife that he was to be served a notice of ejectment as he owed Lord Ardilaun £13, 12s for more than three years of unpaid rent. Under cross-examination by Defense Counsel C. H. Teeling,[43] Kerrigan stated he was in the barn cleaning oats when he saw Joe Huddy:

> On the 3rd of January, I saw Joe Huddy and a boy with him come along the boreen towards my house. I saw three persons follow Joe Huddy and the boy. I knew those persons previously. They were Pat Higgins, Thomas Higgins, and Michael Flynn.

---

[41] In the days leading up to the trial, highly prejudicial and false stories appeared in the newspapers, most particularly the *Times* of London, in which it was reported that John Huddy, the grandson, had been thrown into a sack when he was still alive, "compelling one of the party to carry him on his back to the lake, while the poor boy kicked and struggled in vain to escape." ("Ireland," December 4, 1882)

[42] Kerrigan testified that he had been a tenant of the Guinness family for twenty-six years, but that is incorrect. According to Griffith's valuation, in 1857, Kerrigan was a tenant of Lord Leitrim. It is likely that Lord Ardilaun acquired Upper Cloughbrack when he purchased parts of the Ross estate in 1875.

[43] C. H. Teeling and co-counsel Richard Adams told Justice O'Brien that they had not been "retained" by the accused but rather "assigned," by whom is not stated. In a speech given in Manchester, Michael Davitt stated that Teeling was a poor, office-seeking, miserable "Castle hack," that is, someone in the employ of Dublin Castle. Despite Davitt's low opinion of Teeling, he vigorously represented the accused.

The prisoner came up behind Joe Huddy and struck him on the head with a stone and knocked him down, and gave him two kicks while on the ground. The other two men came up and put shots into his body. The boy ran along the boreen, Michael Flynn followed him, caught him by the collar of the coat, and knocked him down. Thomas Higgins then came up and fired shots at the boy. The old man, Joe Huddy, was put into the basket [a creel used to carry peat]. The prisoner took it away with him. When Joe Huddy was knocked down, I saw my wife coming out of our house with water to throw on the street [an open space beside the house], and my youngest son, Martin, coming out of the house with a basket to me. My son, Mathias [Matthew], returned from the bog exactly when the boy was being killed. When the little boy had been put into the sack, my son Mathias was caught by Thomas Higgins, who told him to carry the sack away. My son was standing in the yard afraid to go. Thomas Higgins said to him "Stand up here or I will make you sorry." The bodies were taken down the boreen... My son came back after an absence of three-quarters of an hour.

When questioned about the bag that held the body of the young Huddy, Kerrigan admitted that it was his, but, pointing to the prisoner, said: "There is the man who took the bag from my house." When asked by Teeling if he had anything to do with the murder, Kerrigan replied: "No more than any man in this court… Neither had my son nor my wife anything to say to it. My wife was not arrested, but my eldest son Mathias [Matthew] was arrested for the murder and kept in prison for about three weeks afterwards. I had known Michael Flynn for over twenty years. I knew Thomas Higgins since he was born. There is no doubt but both were there that morning."

Bridgit Kerrigan (with husband Mathias in the sketch on page 79) was called to the witness box to testify. A description of Mrs. Kerrigan appeared in a transcript of the ninth day of the Parnell Commission in September 1888. It is not flattering: "Mrs. Kerrigan then stepped into the box. A short, squab-figured, dumpy little woman she was, with the face of *Punch's* typical Hibernian. She wore a bright tartan shawl over her head in the manner of Irish peasant women. Holding a red handkerchief to her chin, she fixed her elbow on the ledge of the box as she gave her story in a guttural Erse babble as rapid as her husband's."

At the time of the Huddy trials, a wife's testimony required confirmation from another party, but once confirmation was provided, in this case, by the teenaged Kerrigan sons, the jury was at liberty to consider the evidence of the wife and not to exclude it from consideration.

Bridgit Kerrigan corroborated everything her husband had stated under oath, including that she had seen Patrick Higgins, her first cousin and nearest neighbor, strike Joe Huddy with a stone at the back of her house. She also testified that she knew her husband was to be served with an ejectment decree for the January petty sessions because Mr. Burke, Ardilaun's agent,  had told her so, but she did not know what day it was to be served. She then stated that she had the rent money, more than thirteen pounds, ready for Huddy when he came, which would have been an enormous sum to have had in her possession. She was aware that Joseph Huddy was Lord Ardilaun's bailiff.

Matthew Kerrigan, fifteen, testified that he was returning from the bog "with a load of turf on the back of an ass" for his breakfast when he saw brothers-in-law, Thomas Higgins and Michael Flynn of Middle Cloughbrack, at the back of the barn:[44]

> They were right over the boy murdering him with shots. Thomas Higgins was firing the shots. Pat Higgins, the prisoner, was standing in the boreen a little distance off... The prisoner and Michael Flynn put it [Joe Huddy] into a basket. The prisoner hoisted the basket on the back of Michael Flynn, and they both went down the boreen towards the lake. The boy's body was put into a sack [taken from the Kerrigan house]. The witness said he would not. Tom Higgins said if he did not, he would not be thankful. Witness then carried the sack as far as

---

[44] Thomas Higgins was Michael Flynn's brother-in-law as Tom's sister Bridgit had married Michael Flynn around 1864. Together, they had seven children: six sons and one daughter, all of whom immigrated to the United States four years after Michael Flynn's execution.

Michael Corbett's house, out of which Pat Mannion came. Tom Higgins then tripped Mannion, and the body was put on Mannion's back, and he was told to carry it, and he carried it to the house of Patrick Higgins (Sarah). Then Tom Higgins hoisted the bag on Patrick Higgins (Sarah), and they went out of sight. There was a great hill between witness and the lake, and they left his view.[45]

Eleven-year-old Martin Kerrigan confirmed his parents' account of the murders. He also swore that he had seen revolvers in the hands of Thomas Higgins and Michael Flynn.

Patrick Mannion, an older man, testified that when he came out of the home of Michael Corbett, he saw, in the boreen, Tom Higgins, Pat Higgins, and Matthew Kerrigan. The young Kerrigan had a bag on his back. Tom Higgins came up to him and told him, "Walk out here." When Mannion said that he would not, Higgins "fell on him and tripped him. He pulled him after him on the road. He took the bag off young Kerrigan's back and put it on Mannion's back and told him to walk out. Mannion said he was not able to walk out. He carried it for a little [but when turning the corner on the barn] fell under it. It was then that Patrick Higgins (Sarah) took it off him." In his emotional testimony, Mannion recounted his desire to escape, his twice tripping, the horror of seeing the boy's shoes sticking out of the sack, and Tom Higgins walking behind him holding the bottom of the sack to keep the boy from falling out.

Although Patrick Mannion's testimony was emotionally compelling, the person on trial for his life was Patrick Higgins, and in cross-examining the Mannions, defense counsel succeeded in eliciting testimony from both Patrick and Tom Mannion that at no time had they seen Patrick Higgins commit a criminal act. Quite the contrary, Patrick Mannion stated that Higgins stood "convenient to his own house doing nothing at all."

---

[45] According to Irish author Katherine Tynan, who lived in the area, Joseph Huddy "died game." "Some of the men had revolvers, and they fired them into Joe… At the first shot he fell, sitting down, on the dunghill. While the fellows were loading the revolvers again, Joe kept calling out to them in Irish: 'Come on again, ye divil!' And so till they finished him." Obviously, the story grew more interesting in the retelling.

Two men, John "Luke" Holleran and his son John, swore that when they looked over their garden gate, they saw Patrick Higgins "a little removed from his own house, looking down the boreen." They also stated that they were in their barn when they heard shots fired. When they went into the boreen to find out what had happened, they saw Kerrigan "simply standing with his hands by his side."

The second day of the trial was dedicated to the cross-examination of two witnesses: Kate Higgins, daughter of the accused, and Mary Conroy, a girl from Middle Cloughbrack. After being examined by defense counsel, Kate Higgins was cross-examined by Solicitor General for Dublin, George Bolton. Any progress defense counsel had made on Higgins's behalf was greatly damaged by Kate's testimony, who began by stating that she was "over 12 years of age, and I don't know how much more."

When interviewed by Magistrate Brady and Prosecutor Bolton in September, Kate had stated that she was miles away from the scene in Glenlusk, five miles south of Upper Cloughbrack, at the time of the murders visiting the Collins family. Mary Conroy had told these same men that she had been at school the day of the murders. However, when questioned by the Crown Prosecutor, rather than attending school, Mary swore that she had gone to the Higgins house on that day to help Mrs. Higgins card wool. When she arrived, Mrs. Higgins was not ready for her, and she agreed to help Kate with the oats. In her courtroom testimony, Kate stated that, rather than being miles away in Glenlusk, she had been carrying sheaves of corn (the generic name for all grains) from the field into the barn of Patrick Higgins (Long) who was threshing it. Obviously, Kate could not be in two places at one time. In court, she testified that:

> She was drawing corn [oats] with her father on that day from early in the morning until after dark—the whole day, and he never left her… The Huddys did not come to the house to serve processes or any other business… After hearing the shot, she first threw her load of oats down in the barn, and then ran out to see what was the matter. The dead men were lying in the boreen. She was going afterwards across the road with geese, when Matthew [Mathias] Kerrigan said to her: "If you do not go out of that, I will do the same to you as I did to those men." Kerrigan was at his own door at that time, and a girl named

Mary Conroy was along with witness. She saw Kerrigan and his son putting a man into a bag. She ran back and told her father. It was not then that her father came out for the first time. It was before she drove the geese down the boreen that he saw the bodies and the Kerrigans and blessed himself. She knew Michael Flynn and Thomas Higgins but did not see either of them there.

Even before the Crown Prosecutor went on to shred Kate's credibility, there were problems with her testimony. Mr. J. H. Ryan, who had overseen the making of the model and maps, testified that "It was impossible for Kate Higgins from the point on the boreen where she said she stood, to have seen bodies lying where she alleged she saw the bodies of the Huddys." Joseph Huddy's body was on the boreen while his grandson's body was on the street (the yard on the gable end of the Kerrigan house). After Ryan's testimony, the Crown attacked the integrity of the witness. Kate made their task all the easier when she stated that she had not been deposed in her home by Resident Magistrate Brady and Crown Prosecutor Bolton when she most definitely had been. Records showed that on October 4, 1882, the two men had gone to the home of Patrick Higgins in Upper Cloughbrack and had interviewed his daughter Kate. Mr. Brady had taken down the evidence given by Kate Higgins, after which, she had put her mark on it.

According to Kate, she had no memory of giving any information to Mr. Brady or Mr. Bolton in her home. When Justice O'Brien asked the men to stand up, Kate stated that she had not seen either of them in her house, she had not given information about the Huddy murders to them, she had not kissed a book after swearing, nor had she sworn that she was the daughter of Pat Higgins (Long). "She had never taken an oath in her life."

The Crown then challenged her on her deposition, line by line:

"Did you swear, 'I was at Glenlusk the morning the Huddys were killed?'" – "No; I said something to the police that I was not at home for fear they would take me with them."

"Did you say you were in Glenlusk on a visit at the house of a man named Stephen Collins, and you left after breakfast and returned about the fall of evening?" – "No."

"Did you say, 'When I left the house that morning, I left my father and brother behind me threshing oats?'" – "No."

"Did you say, 'My mother was in the house also tying the straw?'" – "No."

"Did you swear, 'I did not hear of the murder of the Huddys, until the police were looking for them?'" – "No."

"Did you swear, 'No stranger came into our house that morning?'" – "No."

"Then you did not swear anything whatever, nor put your mark to any paper whatever on the 4th of October or any other time, and you never kissed the book until you kissed it here to-day?" – "Never."

Kate's testimony strains credulity. Despite shots being fired in the yard of the house across the boreen from his own, Patrick Higgins showed no curiosity when his daughter ran into the barn raising the alarm. Even when Kate told him there were bodies lying in the boreen, his only reaction was to say that he didn't know who the dead men were even though the process servers had been in the village that very morning and had served several of his neighbors, and Joseph Huddy was known—and despised—throughout the district.[46]

It was obvious Kate was lying, but it is easy to imagine why. Twelve-year-old Kate Higgins sat alone, on a raised platform, in a witness chair, facing a bewigged judge, robed barristers, and an all-male jury, all of whom were much more clever than she was. Looking at her father, guarded by police officers, she understood that her father's life might very well depend on her testimony, and as such, she would say whatever was necessary to secure his freedom.

Things went better for Patrick Higgins when seventeen-year-old Mary Conroy was called to testify and gave her evidence in English. Mary's account was similar to that of Kate Higgins. After hearing a loud noise (shots being fired), Kate and Mary went into the barn and told Patrick Higgins what they had heard. He told them to find out

---

[46] The *Freeman's Journal* of December 14, 1882 reported that Kate testified at this first trial that Mathias and Matthew Kerrigan had carried the bodies of Joseph and John Huddy down the boreen to the lake, a statement she denied making at the second trial.

what it was all about. Both girls ran to the top of a hillock and saw the Kerrigans moving around the bodies, after which, they went back to the barn and told Patrick that they had seen bodies lying on the boreen. He responded by saying that he did not know who the dead men were but wondered where the Kerrigans would hide their bodies. He thought they might bury them on his farm or another's to thrown blame on someone else.[47] Mary was able to point out on the model the position of the bodies—exactly where the Kerrigans had placed them—thus confirming the evidence of the Crown and contradicting Kate Higgins.

The task of addressing the jury fell to defense counsel Richard Adams. He had to deal with the fact that the daughter of Patrick Higgins had lied—repeatedly—and although not specifically mentioned in the newspaper accounts, apparently Mary Conroy had also been caught in "a fine lie" as well. Adams did his best:

> Although the witnesses for the defence had left the table [a raised platform around which the attorneys and prosecutors sat] somewhat under a cloud, for not having told the truth on a former occasion to the magistrate, yet they must believe that the evidence of those girls established this at least, that Patrick Higgins (Long) did not commit the murder. Even if they told the magistrates ten thousand lies regarding themselves, they told the truth now, when they said that Patrick Higgins, the prisoner, was in the barn when the murder was committed... If their evidence was to be rejected on the ground he had mentioned, then upon the same ground the evidence of every witness for the Crown was not trustworthy, for all of them had during the nine months of Kerrigan's imprisonment made many statements to the police, declaring that they knew nothing of the deed.

Remarkably, when the bodies were recovered from the lake, several of the ejectment decrees were found intact on John Huddy.[48] When Justice O'Brien addressed the jury, he stated that although the original

---

[47] At this time, criminal defendants did not appear in their own defense.

[48] The *Guardian* reported that a member of the jury saw evidence of heavenly intervention by the murdered grandson in that the ejectment decree for Kerrigan had been found on his body, thus "The young Huddy spoke from his grave to the fact that he had served the copy."

of Kerrigan's notice of ejectment had been found on the body, the copy was missing, implying that Kerrigan had been served.

> Having referred in detail to the several notices found on the body, and pointing out the various discrepancies which appeared in contradiction to the arguments of counsel, his lordship [O'Brien] continued to say that in the case of Mathias Kerrigan, the original of the civil bill of ejectment was found on the person of the elder Huddy, and a strong argument, at least considered so by the prisoner's counsel, was advanced to prove the serving on him of the civil bill. It had been advanced that that service had taken place and that the receipt of that civil bill and the danger of resulting eviction supplied a strong and sufficient motive for Mathias Kerrigan committing this awful crime, and also that the absence of that civil bill copy, taken in conjunction with the statement made by him on oath that he did not receive such, was evidence…to cast on him the imputation of perjury.

But then Judge O'Brien went on to suggest that "in the confusion and haste that occurred at the time and the circumstances attending it, the document may have been taken away indifferently among many others without any special reason at all."

Justice O'Brien, in instructing the jury, had provided a way out for Kerrigan, but not so for Patrick Higgins, the accused:

> This was the last day for the service of these writs and they had the line taken by him traced by the service of these writs. [Huddy] had a civil bill to be served on Pat Higgins, and in the ordinary course of his duty, he would be required to serve it on that day. Yet no service was made, according to the daughter's evidence. It amounted to an absolute certainty—at least a reasonable certainty, in the learned Judge's mind that the civil bill was served on Pat Higgins, and in his opinion, that circumstance outweighed any evidence, not to speak of the evidence of his own daughter, which, for reasons which were fresh in their memory, should be altogether laid out of this case. Joseph Huddy had not reached the place to effect the service of that civil bill on Mathias Kerrigan, but he had actually made the service at the house of Higgins as he passed. All the evidence leading to the assumption was entirely without contradiction.

Now, passing away from that for the present, [Justice O'Brien] would look at the case as presented by the Crown. He could not himself see how the question of law as to accomplices had any application to this case at all. An accomplice was a person who took part with others in the execution of crime… But, so far from producing Kerrigan as an accomplice, the Crown had brought him forward as innocent of criminal connexion with the crime with which the prisoner stood charged, and his evidence had been fully supported by witnesses who had no connexion or interest with him. The case for the Crown was clearly proved, while that for the defence was supposed by evidence of a most unsatisfactory and false character.

Justice O'Brien's bias in favor of the Crown's case and the guilt of Patrick Higgins is stunning when seen through modern eyes. But at the time of the trial, there was a widespread belief that the increase in violence in Ireland was not a series of isolated incidents, but, rather, the work of outside provocateurs. Justice O'Brien stated: "It was plain that this was not a crime arising out of sudden provocation or out of sudden anger. It was plainly a crime committed with the aid of 'external agencies;' that is, the Land League—an organization that had stirred up memories of ancient wrongs that were now to be remedied by murder, if necessary—or 'trained hands,' aka, a secret society."

If Patrick Higgins were to be found not guilty, it was necessary for his defense counsel to implicate another, and that "other" was Mathias Kerrigan. Following the judge's lead regarding external agencies, Teeling insisted that Kerrigan "was a leading member of the Land League in its most advanced state…[and] made the object of the bounty, consideration, and approval of that organization… The clothes he received in prison were not supplied by the Government or by the police; but from the Land League…the same Land League that was responsible for three-fourths of the crime committed within the last few years in this country."[49] He reminded the jury that the murders had

---

[49] Kerrigan's clothes, a waistcoat and a coat, were provided by the Ladies' Land League headed by Charles Stewart Parnell's sister Anna. In addition to donating clothes to prisoners, the ladies provided small sums of money to sustain families of those arrested for agrarian crimes. In the case of the Kerrigans, it was one pound per

taken place "at Kerrigan's door and at nobody else's" and that the police "with unerring instinct" had arrested Kerrigan and not Patrick Higgins.

In instructing the jury, Justice O'Brien stated that Thomas Higgins and Michael Flynn were "strangers in this locality." That statement was demonstrably false as Mathias Kerrigan had stated under oath that he had known Thomas Higgins "from the time he was born and Michael Flynn, a neighbor, for over twenty years." In light of these connections, O'Brien's instructions were based on a falsehood:

> It was plain that this was not a crime arising out of sudden provocation or out of sudden anger. It was plainly a crime committed with the aid of external agencies; such agency the evidence of Kerrigan and his family fairly established. The life of the elder Huddy and that of his young grandson were taken away by revolver bullets. Not less than seven shots were proved to have been discharged into the bodies of these two men. Thomas Higgins and Michael Flynn *were strangers to this locality,* and it was a significant fact that they had used revolvers. The case had been tried all through as if the object of the crime had been the prevention of the service of these writs. That might have been, but unfortunately the state of things then existing in the country, and the evidence given before them, pointed at the crime as being something not merely done for this purpose, or for the benefit of an individual, but rather as a part of the working of a general organization for the purpose of making general war on the officers of the law. [Again, the inference is that these men were doing the Land League's bidding.]
>
> If Thomas Higgins and Michael Flynn came there and had revolvers, and had used them on that morning, they had not come there, strangers, for the single purpose of preventing the service of these writs. They had come with a more deadly and deliberate purpose. Was it possible, or conceivable, or credible, according to their experience and observations, that Mathias Kerrigan, his wife, his sons, one 15 and the other eight [thirteen], should be there alone, as the daughter [Kate Higgins] of the prisoner had sworn, firing revolver shots into those dead

---

month. No physical evidence was presented to show that Kerrigan even belonged to the Land League.

bodies, or that they could carry these bodies away in the manner described, and taking them out in boats, bury them in the waters of Lough Mask?

Justice O'Brien could not view the matter in any other light: Strangers Thomas Higgins and Michael Flynn were affiliated with an "external agency" (the Land League) and were "trained hands" (assassins under orders from a secret society) as evidenced by their appearance in the Kerrigans' yard early that January morning with revolvers.

In the Judge's charge to the jury, Justice O'Brien stated that "The evidence of John Halloran [sic] pointed clearly to assistance being forthcoming from entirely foreign and external agency." It can be surmised from that statement that Holleran had testified to an affiliation by both Thomas Higgins and Michael Flynn in a secret society. It should be noted that after his release from Galway City Jail, Mathias Kerrigan stayed with the Holleran family.

O'Brien characterized the testimony given by Higgins's daughter as "wholly and wickedly false." He added the weight of his office to that declaration when he stated that "The evidence of the Kerrigans and the other Crown witnesses were entirely uncontradicted by any truthful testimony."

In these clearly biased instructions to the jury, Justice O'Brien made no mention of the sheer stupidity of Thomas Higgins and Michael Flynn in executing the Huddys in broad daylight, with numerous witnesses present. As agents of a clandestine "external agency," shouldn't they have been more careful and clever than that? That was a possibility O'Brien never addressed.

One hour and four minutes later, the jury foreman returned saying that they had a hung jury, and there was nothing to be done about it. Apparently, there was one holdout, the sole Catholic on the jury, and he would not budge on his "no" vote. A new trial was put on the docket for a week Monday.

Chapter 11
Second Trial
of Patrick Higgins

The second trial of Patrick Higgins began on December 13, 1882. The fact that only one juror had voted for acquittal at his first trial did not bode well for Higgins, but his counsel, C. H. Teeling and Richard Adams, put up a spirited defense, consisting mostly of trying to prove that Mathias Kerrigan had perjured himself and that he was, in fact, the man who had murdered the Huddys. In a curious attempt to clear his client, Teeling painted a grim picture of the Irish landscape: "The service of an ejectment process was a recognized motive, at all events amongst certain bodies of tenantry, for the commission of murder." In that statement, Teeling had unwittingly provided a motive for his client: Patrick Higgins had been served an eviction notice on January 3rd.

Counsel requested that Justice O'Brien rule on the proposition that if Kerrigan was found to have perjured himself on one point, that is, the receipt of the notice of ejectment, that the judge must caution the jury that any evidence provided by said witness was "open to the gravest suspicion," and that the jury was entitled to disregard his testimony because jury deliberations must be based on "truthful evidence." The judge consented.

Defense made the point that it was Kerrigan who had much to lose if Joseph Huddy was successful in serving a notice of ejectment. "Unless Kerrigan could destroy the evidence of the service of the process, he would in 16 days be liable to eviction. There was no way of destroying that evidence save by destroying the bailiff who had served it." Counsel reminded the jury that the murder had been committed "at the gable of [Kerrigan's] own house, in his own presence, in the presence of his family…and the sack which was to form the coffin of one of the murdered persons was his sack… Had not Mathias Kerrigan the most awful temptation to act so that he might remove the halter from his own neck and place it round the neck of another."

Counsel further reminded the jury that Kerrigan had been held for nine months in the jail in Galway City. If he were innocent, why had he waited nine months before providing the police with evidence that the murders had been committed by others?

Defense then introduced evidence from the doctor who had examined Joseph Huddy. Kerrigan had sworn that Huddy had first been knocked down by Higgins with a stone to the back of his head, but there was no evidence on the body of such an injury. (See Notes for autopsy results.) In response to the Crown's suggestion that Huddy might have been wearing a top coat and that the coat would have cushioned the blow, defense counsel stated that Huddy must have been wearing the coat on the top of his head in order for no bruise to show. Dr. Hegarty testified that "There was no wound on Huddy's skull to indicate that he was knocked down with a stone. He could not say from the situation of the wounds whether they were all caused by one person."

Finally, counsel for Higgins reminded the jury that although the original process for Kerrigan had been found on the body of Joseph Huddy, the copy was missing. The implication was that Kerrigan had been served, thus the motive for the murders.

It is not possible to know if Adams and Teeling's defense was having a positive impact on the jury. What can be learned from newspaper coverage is that the testimony of the accused's daughter, Kate Higgins, was a disaster. When questioned by the Crown prosecutor, she stuck to the testimony given at the first trial—that after hearing the shots, she had gone into the barn to tell her father what she had heard. "Her father said nothing."

> Prosecutor: "Never asked what the shots were?" – "They suspected something was going on wrong?"
>
> "But he never stirred from his work?" – "No."
>
> "Then you and Mary Conroy went out to the boreen?" – "Yes."
>
> "What did you see?" – "I saw Kerrigan and his wife and children and two men murdered."

The witness then pointed out where the two bodies were. She could not say which body was which.

> "Did you swear on Friday last that both bodies were lying together, side by side, on Kerrigan's street?" – "I was not put to my oath whether that was the spot or not."
>
> "Whether you were put to your oath or not, did you point out that as the spot?" – "I did not. I did not hear Mary Conroy examined on Friday. She is living in Dublin. I don't know the name of the house. I am sleeping in the same room with her."
>
> "Did Mary Conroy tell you since Friday that the one body was on the boreen and the other at the end of the house?" – "She did not."

When one considers the atmosphere of violence existing in the country, as well as the assassinations of Lord Frederick Cavendish and William Burke in Phoenix Park earlier in the year, it is unlikely that anything or anyone could have saved Patrick Higgins from the hangman. His daughter's testimony—that she had said one thing when first interviewed and another in court—was decidedly unhelpful. When questioned under oath, she stated that she "did not think it was any harm to swear a lie except in a court. She looked at the book she was asked to kiss on that occasion to see if there was a cross on it. There was none, so she thought it was no harm to swear a lie on it." In his charge to the jury, Justice O'Brien declared that twelve-year-old Kate had committed perjury. It is likely that her youth saved her from prosecution.[50]

The testimony of Kate Higgins served to reinforce the impression that the whole village of Upper Cloughbrack had either participated in the murders and/or helped in the disposal of the bodies or were part of a conspiracy of silence; that is, they deliberately withheld information to thwart the investigation. The Crown specifically mentioned the two Hollerans, the Mannions, and Mary Conroy as being part of that conspiracy.

---

[50] The Bible, a fixture in Protestant homes, did not exist in the homes of Catholic peasants. All scriptural teachings came from the Gospels and Epistles as read during the Mass by a Roman Catholic priest. This might explain the ease with which Kate lied after kissing a Bible—a book that would have been unknown to her.

In summation, Mr. Adams urged the jury not to return a verdict of guilty "unless they were certain of his guilt as they were of their own existence... If, after fully considering the case, they were only in the mental condition of Festus when confronted by Paul, 'almost persuaded,' they were bound to acquit him."

After the jury retired, Teeling asked Justice O'Brien to recall the jury to tell them that when the judge had said that "It was inevitable that the prisoner was served with an ejectment process," that that was his opinion and not a conclusion of law, and they were at liberty to disagree with the judge. Although the jury was recalled, the seed had been planted in the minds of the jury that an eviction notice had been served on Higgins, and such service was a powerful motive for murder.

After one hour's deliberation, Higgins was found guilty.

When the prisoner, who spoke not a word of English, was told by his interpreter of the verdict, he knelt several times and extended his arms, after which, he requested permission to address the court: "Before God and the Virgin, I never lifted hand or foot or anything else on that man, and I leave it to the Court to do what they like with me."

* * *

In his charge to the jury, Justice O'Brien had stated that it was his opinion "that Higgins was the least guilty of the three persons concerned in the murder, and that the evidence has produced in my mind a firm belief that the design of this murder did not originate with him."

Without a doubt, the judge's comments regarding Higgins being less guilty than the two other men, who were then in Kilmainham Jail awaiting trial, were prejudicial to the upcoming trials of Thomas Higgins and Michael Flynn, especially when one considers that at least two of the jurors were to serve on all three trials. Mr. Power, foreman of the jury, although overcome with emotion, had been requested by his fellow jurors to tell the court that they concurred with the judge in that Higgins was the least guilty of the three, but they did not go the extra step of recommending mercy.

The following year, in an address before Parliament, William O'Brien, Member of Parliament from Mallow, Cork, railed against packed juries where Catholics were rarely allowed to serve and specifically addressed Justice O'Brien's comments at the trial of Patrick Higgins:

> The only duty of the Judge on the conclusion of the trial was simply to have pronounced sentence. The learned Judge [O'Brien], before pronouncing sentence [in the Maamtrasna murder trial], said that as the prisoner did not understand the English language and as there were other persons to be tried on the same charge, he would refrain from making any observations. Nothing could have been fairer than that. In another case [the Patrick Higgins' trial], however, tried immediately afterwards, the same Judge behaved very differently. "Agreeing as I do in the justice and honesty of the verdict of 'Guilty' that has been found by the jury, I consider it my duty to state that in my opinion the prisoner is the least guilty of the persons concerned in this matter." Now, the only other persons to whom the slightest suspicion attached were the two prisoners who remained to be tried, and who were declared by the informer to have been the principals in the crime. On the trial of the second prisoner, *two jurors who had endorsed the Judge's expression of opinion were among the jury* [emphasis mine]. Of course, they were compelled to convict. When such proceedings as those took place, when Judges were prejudiced and juries packed, there could not be said to be little point in the word applied to the court by one prisoner: "This place is no better than a slaughterhouse."

Despite reservations by judge and jury, there would be no prison sentence for Patrick Higgins. Higgins, a father of six children, two in America, two in England, and two at home,[51] was to be conveyed to the jail in Galway City where he would be hung by the neck until he was dead. The date of execution was set for January 15, 1883.[52]

---

[51] The only son of Patrick Higgins living at home was away from Upper Cloughbrack on the day of the murders.

[52] Because Justice O'Brien did not don the black hat when passing sentence on Patrick Higgins, as he did for Michael Flynn and Thomas Higgins, and because he had assigned a different date for his execution from that of the two other men convicted of the murders, a shred of hope remained for Higgins and his family that

The *New York Times* reported that "William Marwood, the executioner, has arrived here [in Dublin] on his way to Galway. He is escorted by nine detectives."

The verdict in the trial of Patrick Higgins foretold the fates of Thomas Higgins and Michael Flynn, but it was necessary for the Crown to go through the motions of a fair trial.

---

his sentence might be commuted. "The Lough Mask Murders – No Reprieve," *Belfast Morning News*, January 15, 1883

Chapter 12
Trial of Thomas Higgins

Thomas (Tom) Higgins, a tenant farmer from Middle Cloughbrack, was described as a dark-haired young man, dressed in tweed, of about twenty-five years of age. He sported a moustache and "a quick eager look." He wore a blue cloth coat and vest and around his neck was a red and white woolen scarf. He spoke only a little English.

The trial began on December 15, 1882 with Crown Prosecutor. James Murphy, Q. C., stating the obvious: The jurors had general knowledge of the facts of the case and the results of the two trials of Patrick Higgins. They were also aware that Higgins had been found guilty as such reports were widely broadcast throughout Dublin and the country. However, he was "perfectly certain" that the jurors would be able to disregard all they had seen and heard and render a just verdict.

Murphy shared the findings of the post mortem: The elder Huddy had received five gunshot wounds and the grandson two. An investigation of the site had found a bullet mark on part of the wall of Kerrigan's house and another on the wall of the boreen.

Crown witness Mathias Kerrigan repeated the testimony he had given at the trials of Patrick Higgins:

> Kerrigan was in his barn when he saw the two Huddys coming up the boreen, and three men coming after them, Pat Higgins (Long), Thomas Higgins [the prisoner], and Michael Flynn…Pat Higgins struck old Huddy with a stone, and knocked him down. Pat Higgins was not more than the length of his arm from Joe Huddy when he struck him with the stone. Huddy fell against the wall, and the others put shots into him. The moment young Huddy saw the old man down, he ran away, and Michael Flynn followed him, and caught him by the collar and knocked him down on the road. Thomas Higgins then put two shots into him.

The Crown rested.

The defense presented twenty-eight witnesses. As with the trial of Patrick Higgins, witnesses, who were meant to corroborate Tom Higgins's alibi, ended up hurting more than helping. Judy (aka Julia) Holleran, a married sister of the accused, testified that she had arrived at the cottage on Monday, the day before the murder, from Claggan, five miles distant, to get some yarn in order for her husband, a weaver, to complete some frieze, a coarse woolen cloth without a nap worn by the Irish peasantry. As the yarn was not ready, she spent the night in her brother's home. Also present in the home was Tom's wife and their young child of about two. In the morning, a neighbor, Sally Laffy, came to the cottage. When she arrived, Tom was still in bed, and after breakfast, he had a smoke. According to Sally, Tom was in and out of the house all day "drawing potatoes" and that he had not been absent from the house for an interval greater than a quarter of an hour.

The problem with Judy's testimony was that she had her brother engaged in household duties that were uncommon for men "in humble homes" to do: washing potatoes, pouring out the water from the potatoes, and boiling a second pot of potatoes to feed the pigs. The reason Judy Holleran gave for Tom's assistance was that she was in a hurry for the wool, and his wife was working the spinning wheel. The judge was skeptical that in a house in which three women were present that Tom Higgins would have made them breakfast and performed women's work.

The judge had good reason to be skeptical. In Irish peasant homes, separation of the sexes was part and parcel of life in a rural village. Men did manly things, and women did everything else. This self-imposed segregation extended to attendance at church where women and children sat on one side of the aisle and the men on the other, and never the twain shall meet. This was not an uncommon custom in farming communities across Europe, but the Irish Catholic Church went the extra mile to keep the sexes apart. An Irish tradition of dancing at the crossroads was attacked by local priests as dancing might lead to other things. The typical Irish dance, with hands by one's side, came about because throwing one's arms in the air might encourage impure thoughts and lead to other things. Anything that might "lead to other things" was frowned upon. It was for that reason that the Church provided numerous religious rites, rituals, and organizations to keep the peasantry engaged. Most marriages were arranged by a family member or a matchmaker based on every consideration except love.

The judge was also suspicious that Judy Holleran just so happened to be in the house on the day the murders were committed. He stated that the accused's sister "was under a tremendous motive not to tell the truth." Things got worse when Judy could not provide the name of any person who had seen her coming or going to Upper Cloughbrack, implying that she had not been there at all—that her entire testimony was a lie in order to save her brother's life.

The biggest problem with Judy Holleran's testimony was that in a statement made to Sergeant Rudden in her home on October 18, 1882, she had denied being in her brother's house spinning wool on the day of the murders. With this contradiction, it is not surprising that judge and jury viewed her testimony as an effort to save her brother from being convicted of a capital offense.

It was then Sally Laffy's turn to be questioned. She stated that her home was a half mile from Tom Higgins's house. On that Tuesday, she had walked to the Higgins home, and once there, had joined Judy Holleran in spinning. She, too, had seen Tom Higgins going in and out of the house all day "drawing potatoes." Her testimony gave the impression of being rehearsed as she parroted nearly everything Judy Higgins Holleran had said in her testimony.

When cross-examined by Mr. Murphy, Sally Laffy, who had been repeatedly questioned by the police, was reminded by Q. C. Murphy that Police Sergeant Rudden had gone to her house to question her about the murder on October 18, 1882, at which time, Sally had denied that she had been in the prisoner's house at all that day. Rather, she had been in her father's house.

Counsel also reminded her that on the day she had walked to the Clonbur Barracks (about five miles from the Higgins's home) to make a statement, she had been seen talking to Bridgit Holleran, the wife of Tom Higgins on the Clonbur road and had returned home with her. "All this pointed very strongly to some influence being exercised over the young woman Laffy... They could not have a doubt that in the walk to Clonbur Barracks prisoner's wife was in close communication with Sally on the subject of that statement."

Defense Counsel C. H. Teeling's summation before the jury of twelve men insisted that Tom Higgins had no reason to kill the Huddys as he was not one of the people to be served by Joseph Huddy that day. However, that was not the case with the Kerrigans in whose yard the murders had been committed. There was also the testimony of Patrick Mannion, who had actively assisted in the disposal of the body of John Huddy, and his son to be considered. Their original statements were at variance with what they had said in court under oath. But it was on Mathias Kerrigan that Teeling concentrated his fire:

> Mathias Kerrigan had the strongest motive…to commit the crime having regard to the fact that he owed over three years' rent, and that he had been warned that his patient landlord had at last made up his mind that out he should go. Kerrigan swore he was not served with the ejectment by Huddy… The original of the ejectment was found on the body of Joe Huddy, but not the copy, and it was the copy that should be served. Who then had the strongest motive to commit the deed? The prisoner had no motive but if Kerrigan was served with the ejectment that day he knew that out he should go.

Defense counsel reminded the jurors that it had been established in evidence that Bridgit Kerrigan, wife of Mathias Kerrigan, had wiped away traces of blood of the murdered men. Because it was necessary for Kerrigan to deflect blame, he had pointed an accusing finger at Tom Higgins, not knowing that Huddy had no ejectment papers for him. On the morning of January 3rd, Tom Higgins had been "where he ought to be, in his own house, a mile and a half removed from the scene of the murder" in his cottage in Upper Cloughbrack.

Justice O'Brien spent considerable time going over the testimony of the defense witnesses. With regard to Patrick Mannion, "The jury would have to ask themselves why Mannion should have selected the prisoner Thomas Higgins, and not have named some other person as concerned in that crime. His Lordship certainly could not understand why Mannion would do so." In that statement, the judge had given more weight to Mannion's testimony.

Because the body of Joseph Huddy had been brought to the home of Patrick Higgins (Sarah) and Higgins had carried the body at least as far as the lake, Higgins had been named an accessory after the fact, and for that reason, he could not be examined by the Crown as it would have placed him in legal jeopardy. However, it was pointed out by the Crown that Patrick Higgins (Sarah) could have been called as a witness for the defense, and, yet, he was not produced as a witness for Tom Higgins. The reason he was not called is obvious. If called, Higgins (Sarah) would have been subject to cross-examination by both defense *and* the prosecution.

The judge gave various reasons why it had taken Mathias Kerrigan nine months to come forward. He opined that Kerrigan was probably safer in jail, not talking, than to be out of jail implicating his neighbors in the murders. None of the reasons provided by the judge included the possibility that Mathias Kerrigan had actually committed the crime. In fact, the judge stated that ejectment decrees were so common in that part of Ireland that there was no reason for Mathias Kerrigan to resort to such an "atrocious crime" (but it was sufficient motive for Patrick Higgins).

It took the jury one hour and twenty-five minutes to find Thomas Higgins guilty of murder.[53] Before being sentenced, Tom asked to address the court: "I have a few words to say. On my oath I never fired a shot at John Huddy nor Joseph Huddy, or any other man in this world since the day I was born. Yet Kerrigan and his family have sworn falsely. That's all I have to say, gentlemen."

Justice O'Brien donned the black hat and ordered Thomas Higgins to be taken to the Galway City Jail where he was to be hanged by the neck until he was dead. His execution date was set for January 17, 1883.

Now, it was Michael's Flynn's turn.

---

[53] The *Times* of London noted on December 1, 1882: "The special jurors have been summoned to attend [the Green Street Courthouse]. Notwithstanding that they feel *aggrieved* at the transfer of so many cases from the provinces for trial, there is reason to believe that they will not shrink from the discharge of their duty." However, the possibility existed that the "aggrieved" special jurors might render decisions in haste and without proper deliberation because of the number of violent crimes being tried in Dublin by special juries. They had jobs to attend to and homes to go to.

Chapter 13
Trial of Michael Flynn

The trial of Michael Flynn, the last of the three accused to be tried, began on Monday, December 19, 1882, in the Green Street Courthouse before Justice William O'Brien. Flynn was a tenant of Lord Ardilaun and lived in Middle Cloughbrack (America) on a farm at the corner of the Cornamona and Clonbur roads. The *Morning News* of Belfast described the prisoner as "an elderly man, slight in stature, and more impoverished-looking than either his former two prisoners…and was coarsely and roughly dressed in old frieze, without any collar or neckerchief." Despite his humble attire, Flynn had some education, more than Thomas Higgins and Patrick Higgins. It was reported that he spoke both Irish and English and could read and write, but there is no way to determine his proficiency in English—the language of the prosecutors.

While sitting in a corner of the dock, Flynn frequently glanced at the jurors who were to decide his fate. He looked on with wonder at the pageantry of the bewigged and gowned judge and counsel. When jury selection began, Flynn, as had the other defendants, indicated that he would defer to his defense attorney, C. H. Teeling, in making challenges. As was the case with the trial of Thomas Higgins, at least two members of the jury who had rendered a verdict against Thomas Higgins would also determine Michael Flynn's guilt or innocence.

The Solicitor General, Mr. McCaffery, opened the case for the prosecution by referencing the violence now so prevalent in that part of Connemara, including the murder of Lord Mountmorres and the grisly murders of the Joyce family in the Maamtrasna Mountains of Galway (now a part of County Mayo). It was the prosecution's intention to prove that not only was Michael Flynn guilty of the murders of bailiff Joseph Huddy and his grandson John but that he had been the "ringleader and chief." On the morning of January 3, 1882, "the prisoner was seen in the boreen at Kerrigan's house by a lad named [Tom] Mannion. He was in the lane waiting for the Huddys… The prisoner, seeing Mannion, told him he had better go away and get off the boreen. That was a few minutes before the murder."[54]

As with the other trials, there was an attempt by the Crown prosecutors to tie the murders to the Land League. They had been unsuccessful with both of the Higgins men, but with Michael Flynn, they had a more fertile field to plow. Flynn had been a member of the Clonbur branch of the Land League since June 1880. When he was arrested in January 1882, as part of a sweep of the village following the Huddys' disappearance, Flynn had on his person a ticket of membership for the Clonbur branch, a legitimate organization that would not be suppressed until October 1882. In his opening statement, Crown Solicitor McCaffery described Flynn as a "leading man in the neighbourhood, who corresponded with [the Land League] on agrarian subjects." This statement was at odds with the evidence. The card Flynn carried, issued by M. Conway, president, and Edward Jennings, secretary, was for general membership in the Clonbur branch.

McCaffery also mentioned correspondence between Flynn and the Land League, but Flynn had not written letters to the Land League, but, rather, to its sister organization, the Ladies' Irish National Land League, an organization providing assistance to the families of the evicted as well as political prisoners. The ladies had arranged for the sum of £1 per week to be paid to Flynn's wife so that she might provide for her family. Flynn, the father of seven children, wrote to Mary Nally, prison secretary for the Ladies Land League, asking that additional funds be provided as "He could not send his children to school because they were almost naked."

By the time Mary Nally received Flynn's letter, the Ladies' Land League was in the process of being dissolved, their functions assumed by a committee of men under the presidency of Charles Stewart Parnell, and because of the impending dissolution, Mary advised Flynn to write directly to Parnell. That was it! Even though Mr. Gildea, the

---

[54] Tom Mannion had also stated to the police that it was Tom Higgins who had told him to get off the boreen. It is possible that both Flynn and Higgins had ordered Mannion off the boreen.

governor of Kilmainham Jail, had read all of the letters exchanged between the two parties, and saw nothing nefarious in them, that, and Flynn's membership card, was McCaffery's proof of collusion with the Land League.

Defense Counsel Richard Adams emphasized to the jury that the letter sent to Mary Nally had nothing to do with the trial of Michael Flynn. He stated that each case must be judged on its own merits, and the jurors were "to decide upon the guilt or innocence of this man as if they now first heard of the murder of the Huddys." The problem with that is that at least two of the jurors, who had voted to convict, had been on the juries for the trials of Patrick Higgins and Thomas Higgins in which Michael Flynn's alleged role was repeatedly referenced. It is impossible to "unhear" something.

Crown Prosecutor McCaffery thought quite a lot of Michael Flynn. The accused was "just the sort of man to be found patrolling the boreen before the murder, and warning the people to keep away." As Flynn was described as "elderly and slight," it wasn't a robust physical appearance that made Flynn "just that sort of man." So, if it wasn't heft, it must have been Flynn's intellect. After all, he could read and write when few of his neighbors could!

On the day of the murders, Flynn swore that he had been at the funeral of Joe Joyce, but according to McCaffery, the accused "was just the man whom they would expect to have intelligence enough to provide for his own safety, and to prepare evidence that he was elsewhere at the time the murder occurred. Funerals and wakes were very good places for the presence of any person who had taken part in a crime, because they afforded opportunities for abundant observation. It was nothing more than the ingenious and clever device which they might expect from a man like the prisoner." In other words, Flynn had an alibi. McCaffery came to his conclusion despite the fact that Flynn was not among those who were to be served that January morning.

So, where was Michael Flynn on the day of the murder? Thomas Flynn, the prisoner's son, testified in Irish, that he had heard his father "telling his mother the night before the funeral to have his shirts ready. My mother got the breakfast on the morning of the funeral very early. My father put on the clothes he used to wear when going to Mass, and went to the funeral." The prosecutor seemed to doubt that the young Flynn spoke only Irish. McCaffery asked Thomas if he went to school to which Thomas replied: "I don't understand you in English." Defense Counsel Adams pointed out that his would not be the sole example of a son speaking only Irish when the father spoke English, but it is possible that this exchange cast a shadow on the young Thomas's testimony. After being dismissed, Thomas went and kissed his father. Flynn's wife was also in court on the day of their son's testimony.

Patrick Duffy, a middle-aged man, stated that he lived at the opposite extreme from Flynn in Middle Cloughbrack, a village that consisted of about ten houses. "On the day of Joe Joyce's funeral, I got up at day [dawn]; I have no knowledge of the hour. After getting up, I put down a fire; then harnessed an ass and went a mile for a load of turf. I went to the bog by the Cornamona Road. I saw the prisoner passing along the road while I was filling the load of turf." Duffy did not speak to him.

Mary Joyce, widow of Joe Joyce, testified that Flynn had been at her house paying his respects.

Thomas Walsh, who spoke English, stated that he was a blacksmith and a relative of the widow of Joe Joyce. "I was engaged coffining Joe Joyce's remains, and on that morning, saw the prisoner Michael Flynn standing at the gable of the [Joyce] corpse house. I don't know what the hour was… I went to the corpse house after my breakfast, and had not been long there when I saw him. I believe Cloughbrack is seven or eight miles from Crumlin [southwest of Cloughbrack]. I was carrying the corpse, and saw the prisoner on the Connemara [Cornamona] road with the funeral. I saw him again at the graveyard at Clonbur."

Michael Joyce, who lived about a mile from the corpse house, "went there on the morning of the funeral. I was there when the funeral started; it's hard for me to say the hour it started, as I hadn't a watch or a clock. It was more than 10 o'clock when I left my own home, and I had only one mile to walk to the funeral, which started about a quarter of an hour after I arrived. I saw the prisoner before the funeral started. I don't remember that I saw him again until I went to Cornamona [Road], about two miles from the corpse house. The graveyard [Rosshill] is near two miles beyond Clonbur. I stopped at Clonbur and saw prisoner there again."

The accused had one witness who had seen him walking toward Joe Joyce's house. There were at least three witnesses who swore that

Flynn had been seen at the corpse house and again at the cemetery. His son testified that he had on his Sunday shirt for the purpose of going to the funeral. In order for McCaffery's scenario to work, Flynn had to go to Joe Joyce's funeral, return to Cloughbrack, kill the Huddys wearing his Sunday best, and show up at the Rosshill cemetery near Clonbur.

However, there were difficulties for Flynn. As no one had a watch or clock, it was impossible for any of the mourners to accurately pinpoint where Michael Flynn was at any given time. The witnesses admitted that they saw him intermittently at Joe Joyce's house, on the Cornamona Road, and, lastly, at the deceased's interment at the Clonbur cemetery. The problem for Flynn was that no witness had come forward who could account for the whole of his time.

Even though the corpse house was five miles away from the scene of the murders, the Crown Prosecutor rebutted the problem of distance by saying that, by quick walking, the distance between where the funeral procession had started and the scene of the murder might be traversed in forty minutes.

In remarks made before sentencing Flynn, Justice O'Brien asserted that the murders had taken place around 9:00 and that the funeral procession had left Joe Joyce's house between 11:30 and 12:00. It was his opinion that after killing the Huddys, Flynn had made haste to the corpse house to establish his alibi.

Defense counsel again put on a vigorous defense that rested largely on the hope that Mathias Kerrigan would be viewed as the real killer and that he had named Thomas Higgins, Patrick Higgins, and Michael Flynn in order to save his own neck.

There were two oddities in the trials. The first concerned Michael Coyne, the driver of the car, who had picked up the Huddys on the morning of January 3. In one account that appeared in the *Guardian*, the driver stated that when the Huddys failed to appear hours after the agreed-upon time, he had driven to Cornamona and made inquiries of the police about Joseph and John Huddy, and a search immediately ensued.

A second telling had Michael Coyne leaving Joseph and John Huddy on the Cornamona road so that they might begin service with Mary Walsh. After Walsh had been served, the driver waited on the road for their return. According to Katherine Tynan, who attended the trials, in her memoir, *The Middle Years*: "The man that was driving them waited a bit and then quietly drove back to Cong; but said nothing about Joe and the grandson till the hue and cry started and then he told where he'd left Joe. Perhaps he guessed what was going on and thought it wisest to keep out of it; and small blame to him!"

At the time of the trials, with Michael Coyne living in the United States unavailable to testify, the judge dismissed any suggestion that the Coyne might have seen something that would have proved beneficial to the defense. In the judge's mind, the driver's testimony would more than likely have assisted the prosecution in that the driver could have witnessed "preparations or arrangements for perpetration of the crime." Apparently, according to the judge, the carman's abilities of observation extended only to criminal activities and not the goings-on of the innocent.

The second oddity involved Catherine "Kate" Moran, who admitted that she had been served by Joe Huddy on the day of his murder. Kate, who repeatedly argued with her inquisitors, was described as "an adverse and reluctant witness" and "an utterly untruthful woman." Kate testified that, "In the evening a stranger whom she had never saw came in and told her to burn the copy of the process that had been served. I never saw the stranger before or since… And sure I would put my hand into the fire for him." Kate had followed the mystery man's instructions, and in the judge's opinion, had "willfully destroyed evidence."[55]

The identity of the stranger remains unknown, and there is nothing to indicate that any investigation was conducted for the purpose of learning his identity. If the story is true, and Michael Flynn and Thomas Higgins were acting on the orders of a secret society, it is possible that the stranger was also a member of a secret society doing clean-up.

---

[55] The Crown prosecutor believed that if they "had been permitted to pursue that inquiry, they might have found that the circumstances of the destruction of the process would have led to the conclusion that she [Kate Moran] knew a great deal more about that crime than she had disclosed. "Lough Mask Murders, Trial of Third Person," *Dublin Daily Express*, December 21, 1882.

During his instructions to the jury, Justice O'Brien told the jury that they were to give no weight to the Land League membership card found on Michael Flynn. He went to great lengths to recreate the route and the approximate times when Joseph and John Huddy would have been at the various houses serving decrees of ejectment. The judge placed the Huddys at Kerrigan's house at 9:30. If Flynn's witnesses were to be believed, Flynn would have been at Joe Joyce's funeral at that time, but Flynn was not to be believed. After an hour's deliberation, the jury returned with a verdict of guilty.

Unlike the other two defendants, who had declared their innocence in brief statements, Michael Flynn had a lot to say:

> Fair and honest, I am as innocent of that crime as any man of the jury or of the Court. I never took in my hand an instrument to look at it for the purpose of examining it with a view to fire a shot with it no more than the child unborn; nor was I in any boreen or road or street to commit this crime, no more than anyone who swore against me. I hope they will beg the Lord's pardon before whom he was going for the sentence they are getting passed upon me. I was not there that day, nor could I be in it, for I was at the funeral, four miles from my own locality, by fair measure of the way I went that day. I hope to God that Ireland is listening and that Ireland will look to see that my wife and children will not die of hunger…for it is a hard thing that I should be brought out from them when my mother, at the age of four score and some odd years, is without a son living who can procure a dinner for her. It is like bringing one to market and selling one that I might be slaughtered. I am not ashamed or afraid of going before God. That is all I have to say.

The reporter for the *Dublin Daily Express* described Flynn as "subsiding into his usual manner of apparent indifference and leaned upon the rails of the dock looking at the judge." And why would he not? Flynn had known his fate from the time the jury at Patrick Higgins' second trial had returned a verdict of guilty.

After the verdict was rendered, Justice O'Brien also had a lot to say:

> Michael Flynn, you have been found guilty by the jury of this crime, upon such evidence as, notwithstanding your protestations and the aggravated means adopted by you to

conceal the effects of this crime, can leave no doubt in the mind of any rational person of your guilt. (Prisoner, in an undertone, "Thank you.")

It was a most cruel and piteous crime. Two unoffending persons who had done you no wrong, towards whom you had no cause for animosity, left their house upon this 3rd of Jan. (Here the prisoner slowly surveyed the audience, and with great callousness, turned to see those who were sitting in the gallery)—for the purpose of doing their duty…as innocent as that of the humble servant of the Crown who delivers the letters from the post. And upon that occasion they were surprised, unthinking of harm, and cruelly and foully murdered by you and others.

Notwithstanding all the means taken by you—by the mode in which the bodies of the victims were disposed of by this false defence that you prepared beforehand for your designed absence at another place—your plot and crime now stand revealed as clearly as the light that descended upon you.

I do not wish to aggravate the painful position in which you are now placed, standing there; notwithstanding all the influences that led you to this crime, you now stand alone and unfriended. But I cannot avoid saying that you were the principal person in this wicked and murderous plot, and I have no doubt upon my own mind that the aged man Patrick Higgins, who might have been disposed himself to live on terms of peace with his neighbors…was persuaded by you to engage with you in this criminal enterprise.

Although the judge sympathized with the plight of Flynn's family, he placed the blame for the shame his relations would feel for Flynn's "violent and ignominious death" squarely on the convicted man's shoulders." O'Brien hoped that with his death, as well as that of his accomplices, "the state of things which existed in this unhappy country shall cease, and that there shall be an end of all this wickedness which has caused so much misery and bloodshed." As he did with Tom Higgins and Patrick Higgins, after sentencing Flynn to death, Justice O'Brien hoped that Flynn would spend the time left to him in seeking God's forgiveness.

As Flynn turned to leave the dock, he looked up at the gallery and said, "I wish you all a good day." (See "Notes – Chapter 13" for more information on Michael Flynn and his family.)

* * *

After presiding over four murder trials, Justice O'Brien's frustration with the state of things in Ireland in general, and with the people of Upper Cloughbrack in particular, was evident in an address he made to the jury:

> After all the investigations which the Crown had prosecuted, and all the light they could throw upon the case, many of the circumstances remained, even at this moment, entirely unknown and mysterious. How the body of Huddy was carried down to the lake after it left the presence of Patrick Mannion and young Kerrigan; by whom it was carried; how it passed down by the Clonbur public road; by whom it was taken along the road; by whom the means of carrying the bodies over the water and sinking them in the lake were provided; whose boat was employed; who put the stones into the sack and upon the body of the elder man; how many were engaged in it—all these matters remain, at this moment, notwithstanding all the investigations and resources of the Crown, an absolute and entire mystery… It is extremely likely that the means taken to dispose of the bodies were observed by a great many people, and, yet, nobody has come forward.

And so it would remain.

* * *

The *Guardian* reported that on the day the three prisoners were removed from Dublin, they traveled under a strong escort. In the cab, on the way to the railway terminus, Flynn laughed and joked with the policeman who had charge of him. When he arrived at the platform, "He stepped jauntily out of the vehicle, and before being put into the train he exclaimed: 'I will die for Ireland; I am going to die for Ireland.' No responsive cheer was given, and the few people on the platform maintained a profound silence. His hands, like those of the other prisoners were heavily ironed."

This display of bravado evaporated on the journey between Dublin and the Galway City Jail. The interval had proved sufficient for Flynn's thoughts to turn to the hangman's noose that awaited him. Upon their arrival in Galway, the *Morning News* of Belfast reported: "The younger Higgins and the old man bade the crowd good-bye, but Flynn remained silent," calling to mind the words of Samuel Johnson: "Depend upon it, sir, when a man knows he is to be hanged in a fortnight, it concentrates his mind wonderfully."

Chapter 14
The Queen's Justice in Galway

Ireland is full of old unhappy things that strangely shake the heart.
H. V. Morton

When one considers the statements made by Justice O'Brien and the foreman of the jury at the first trial of Patrick Higgins—that he was the least guilty of the three men charged—relations of Higgins had reason to hope that his death sentence might be commuted to life imprisonment, and a plea for the exercise of the Prerogative of Mercy, known as a memorial, was sent to the Lord Lieutenant of Ireland. However, it was not to be as John Poyntz Spencer telegraphed: "The law must take its course."

In a January 16th editorial, the *Guardian* commended the Lord Lieutenant for standing firm in the face of considerable pressure to reprieve Patrick Higgins: "The expiation of the offence by the death of the principal agent in its perpetration must be deemed a wholesome example, and all that remains to be regretted is that those under whose orders—it cannot be doubted—the Huddys were murdered have *not* been brought to justice." Again, the editors of the *Guardian* believed, as did much of Ireland's middle and upper classes, as well as everyone in Britain who wasn't Irish, that so heinous a crime must have been committed under the direct orders of an "external agency," that is, the Land League under Charles Stewart Parnell and his henchmen.

Several factors had worked against a reprieve. First, there was the sense that the Land War had made Ireland a place of perpetual warfare. Informers, or those who acted against the boycott, were beaten or murdered. Bailiffs and land agents had become favored targets for reprisal. There had been several notable assassinations or attempted assassinations of members of the Irish peerage or their employees. The murders, in a public park, of the Chief Secretary to the Lord Lieutenant of Ireland, Frederick Cavendish, who was married to a niece of Prime Minister Gladstone, and Thomas Henry Burke, Permanent Undersecretary for Ireland, had shocked the country. By the time of the Huddy murder trials, "There were parts of Ireland where the queen's writ no longer ran. At the end of the nineteenth century, 11,000 policemen in the Royal Irish Constabulary, housed in 1,600 barracks, were required to maintain the peace."

In County Galway, in the years 1879 and 1880, there were 1,068 acts of agrarian violence that were *reported*. It is impossible to know how many crimes went unreported for fear of retaliation. Early in 1881, all meetings were forbidden in Galway under the Arms Act, and Galway was proclaimed to be in a "disturbed state" in accordance with the provisions of The Coercion Act that had been introduced on January 24, 1881 by William Edward Forster, Chief Secretary for Ireland, for the purpose of dealing with the growth of the Land League. One of its provisions allowed the Government to arrest, without trial, persons reasonably suspected of crime and conspiracy, and one of the casualties of the act was Mathias Kerrigan, who was held without charge in the Galway City Jail for nine months.

As a result of the Land War, "Cases were most commonly moved from the West and South, where the agitation was strongest, to Dublin. It was believed that city juries had less sympathy with the agrarian agitators and were less likely to be under the influence of violent or threatening secret societies." By moving the trial of the three men accused of killing the Huddys from Galway to Dublin, chances for conviction greatly increased because, in Dublin, more Protestants than Catholics served on juries. Jury packing was a well-known fact, and despite ongoing protests from the Catholic majority, little had been done to change the system. The religious imbalance between the accused, who were Catholic, and the Protestants who decided their fate, was certainly true of the juries that rendered guilty verdicts against Thomas Higgins, Patrick Higgins, and Michael Flynn.

The matter of Patrick Higgins not understanding "a word of English" must be taken into account. During one of the trials, a translation was challenged, and Justice O'Brien criticized, not the translator, but the man who had made the objection. There were other instances where the prisoners or witnesses spoke at length in answering a question in Irish only to have the translator answer in a few words.

Was there something in those exchanges that had been lost in translation?

There is also the conduct of Justice William O'Brien to be considered. O'Brien had been a Crown prosecutor for fourteen years before ascending to the bench. The judge was known as "a strong judge with a zealous hatred of crime... His charges to grand juries when going on circuit as Commissioner of Assize were models of nervous eloquence. Their delivery, however, and their pointed references to the public events of the time, were the subjects of severe stricture in the Press and of Parliamentary reference." Irish lawyer Maurice Healey, in his legal memoir, *The Old Munster Circuit*, described O'Brien as someone who "invariably regarded the accused's guilt as self-evident, did everything possible to assist the prosecution, and disregarded the fundamental rule that the jury in determining the accused's guilt or innocence must not hear evidence of any prior convictions." O'Brien's statement that Patrick Higgins was "the least guilty of the three" at the time of his sentencing can be viewed as being highly prejudicial to Thomas Higgins and Michael Flynn.

Events outside the courtroom may have influenced the jury. In August 1882, while the prisoners were incarcerated in Kilmainham Jail, the grisly murder of five members of the John Joyce family took place in Maamtrasna, County Galway, across Lough Mask from Upper Cloughbrack. Several motives were suggested, including a rumor that the murdered man's mother, on a visit to the Upper Cloughbrack to see her son, had allegedly informed the authorities that she had seen where the bodies of the two Huddys had been disposed of in Lough Mask.

Despite evidence that the Maamtrasna massacre was the result of a blood feud and payback, there was almost a desperate attempt on the part of the authorities to tie every murder to agrarian violence and the Land League. The Government's proof was the unsolved murder of Lord Mountmorres, violence associated with the boycott, and contempt for the rule of law. All of these conspired against the three defendants.

The obscenely short length of the jury deliberations raises the possibility that the minds of the jurors had already been made up even before they went into the jury room. The presence of jurors who had already served on the jury of Patrick Higgins's two trials, and had convicted him of murder, surely lessened any hope for Thomas Higgins and Michael Flynn of acquittal. Additionally, it is possible that outside factors influenced the jurors in determining guilt or innocence. The story of the murders of the Huddys had received wide coverage in newspapers in Ireland and England and extensively in Dublin. The editorials in the newspapers with the largest circulation, the *Times* and *Guardian* of London and the *Morning News* of Belfast, had shown a clear bias against the defendants and in favor of "the rule of law."

After sentence was passed, each prisoner was transported from Dublin to Galway City Jail for execution. All three men spent considerable time with their confessors, the Rev. John Greaves, P. P. (parish priest) and the Rev. Redmund Newell, C. C. (Companions of the Cross). The wives and relatives of the condemned were allowed two interviews. Thomas Higgins, who was only twenty-five, was "the most depressed in spirits, and his final interview with his young wife was of the most distressing character."

On January 15, 1883, the day of his execution, Patrick Higgins, attended 7:00 mass in the prison chapel. He was then led from the chapel to the prison yard where members of the press were assembled. He died without making a statement of guilt or innocence.

On the day of Patrick Higgins's execution, Michael Flynn, in a detailed statement, confessed to the murders of John and Joseph Huddy. It is likely that Flynn's decision was heavily influenced by his priest who would have encouraged Flynn to go before the seat of judgment with a clear conscience. In his confession, he admitted his own guilt and declared that Mathias Kerrigan and his family were innocent. However, he denied that the Kerrigans could have witnessed the events they testified to at trial. It is notable that in his final hours, Flynn failed to exonerate either Patrick Higgins or Thomas Higgins. It would appear that in the end, the juries had got it right. Flynn's confession in the hours leading up to his execution revealed that his story about his attendance at the Joyce funeral had been largely fabricated. However, it does not necessarily follow that because the men were guilty of the Huddy murders that they had received a fair trial.[56]

---

[56] A centenarian, who grew up in Upper Cloughbrack, was taught to recite the following poem as a child: "Michael Flynn and Thomas Higgins confessed to their

On January 17th, Thomas Higgins and Michael Flynn attended mass. As they climbed the scaffold, Flynn responded to Father Greaves's recitation of the service for the dead. Neither made a statement. Thomas Higgins left behind a wife and a toddler. [57]Michael Flynn's family, his wife, aged mother, and seven children, would find it necessary to rely on the kindness of relatives and neighbors in order to survive.

The Coercion Acts had done their work, and crime statistics showed a marked decrease in agrarian crime following a bloody year of reprisal and murder. However, all was not as it once was. Mathias Kerrigan had been under continuous police protection from the time he had turned informer, and a police hut, housing eight members of the Royal Irish Constabulary, had been erected just a few yards from his house. Even with police protection, in December 1883, the anniversary month of the Huddy murder trials, Mathias Kerrigan was fired upon in Cong. At the time of his appearance before the Commission investigating Parnell and Crime in 1888, Kerrigan was still receiving police protection. It is likely that he continued to receive such protection for the remainder of his life. He died early in 1898.

---

holy priest. They prayed to God on high that they never did the deed." Local lore insists that an assassin, someone not from the village, actually killed the Huddys. Considering Flynn's confession and the more than seven bullets fired in Kerrigan's yard, that's a stretch, but the story lives on more than 135 years after the murders and demonstrates the power of oral history.

[57] Newspaper accounts report the sex of Thomas Higgins's child as a boy. However, a report on a genealogical site indicates that Tom's child was a girl, Mary, born in 1881.

Chapter 15
Questions about the Huddy Murders

In January 1882, the tenants living in Upper Cloughbrack knew that Lord Ardilaun's bailiff was coming into their village to serve notices of ejectment. They also knew the exact date the process servers would knock on their doors as January 3rd was the last day service could be made in order for the cases to be heard in the January petty sessions. There was no doubt that on that Tuesday morning, Joseph Huddy would be walking the boreen of Upper Cloughbrack with processes in his pockets. In court, Bridgit Kerrigan, the wife of informer Mathias Kerrigan, admitted as much when she testified that she had been told by Mr. Burke, Lord Ardilaun's agent, that he had instructed his solicitors to issue an order of ejectment for her family.

Even more damaging testimony from Mr. Burke was given at the trial of Patrick Higgins. According to the *Guardian*, Mathias Kerrigan had been warned by Lord Ardilaun's agent that because "no settlement of the rent had been received, a process of ejectment would be issued against him for the next sessions, which were to take place on the 19th January." The *Guardian* added that "Mathias Kerrigan knew perfectly well that Huddy, the bailiff to whom the ejectment processes were given in the month of December, must come to serve the processes on the 3d January." If the Kerrigans knew about the eviction notices—and the date they would be served—then everyone in Upper Cloughbrack did as well. It would have been a hard thing to keep secret.

There is nothing in the newspaper accounts of the four trials that would indicate that the men of the village had come together to discuss what they should do when Joseph Huddy came into the village. Crown Prosecutor George Bolton stated in his book on the Huddy murders that 211 people had been questioned in connection with the murders.

It is impossible to believe that 211 people had held their tongues about such a meeting during the course of an investigation that lasted from January through October. It is more likely that Michael Flynn and Thomas Higgins, two men who were not to be served by the Huddys, were given orders by a secret society known to exist in the region to take care of the process-server. On the morning of January 3rd, Michael Flynn and Tom Higgins were on the Cornamona Road, waiting for Huddy, and with revolvers in their pockets, they walked the boreen to the Kerrigan farm for the purpose of executing Joseph Huddy.[58]

It is also known that someone from the village had revealed to the police the approximate location as to where the bodies could be found in Lough Mask. Although newspaper accounts described the informer as an "old woman," it was not she who had revealed the names of the killers. So, who did?

Mathias and Bridgit Kerrigan were the parents of four children who were then living at home. On the morning of the murders, Matthew was in the bog gathering turf, and Martin was in the house with his mother. Apparently, fourteen-year-old Bridgit Kerrigan was not in the house at the time of the murders and appears to have played no role in the investigation or trials. But where was older daughter Mary? Family lore has it that Mary was in the hills above the village with the family cow and that she had witnessed the Huddys being murdered. Her grandson, the late Dr. Joseph Lydon, provided me with the family version of what happened next:

> There was another woman who, from her adjacent hillside, saw the bodies thrown into the lake. My grandmother did not see this part of the action, but the second woman from her position had heard the initial commotion and saw Mary Kerrigan in the distance witnessing the fray. It was properly presumed that the bodies were thrown into the loch and a dragging search was initiated at the site. They were about to give up, when the second woman, who had seen the bodies being thrown in with whatever stone weights had been attached, came forward and said: "Search here!" designating the spot. Immediately she

---

[58] According to local historian, Father Jarlath Waldron, "Neighbouring townlands did indeed have a group resembling a Secret Society, Clonbur had one, so had Cornamona, Maam, Leenane, Cloughbrack, and Finney." (*Maamtrasna*, p. 18)

testified that she had seen the disposition but denied having seen or having had anything else to do with the murders. She did state, however, that she had heard the fracas up the road and noted that Mary Kerrigan was standing on her hill, and from that point of view, must have seen the whole episode.

In Dr. Lydon's retelling, there is an element of truth as it mentions the "old woman" who had told the police where the bodies could be found.

According to Dr. Lydon, Mary Kerrigan was questioned by the police but refused to appear as a witness because she doubted the honesty of the interpreter in translating her Irish thoughts into English words. It is true that Mary did not appear as a witness at the trials in Dublin, but it is *not* true that she said nothing when interviewed in Clonbur.

On September 24th, in Clonbur, fifteen witnesses were interviewed by Resident Magistrate A. Newton Brady. On September 25th, Brady was once again back in Clonbur, but this time he interviewed only one person: Mary Kerrigan. In that interview, Mary admitted that she had seen the Huddys walking down the boreen in the direction of her house. But where had Mary been standing when she had seen the Huddys nearing her family home?

During the interviews of the previous day, had one or more of the witnesses revealed that Mary had been in the hills above Upper Cloughbrack with a view of the boreen and the Kerrigan house? It should be remembered that her interrogator, Resident Magistrate A. Newton Brady, along with George Bolton, had knowingly withheld information from the defense at the Maamtrasna trials in order to secure murder convictions for the massacre of the John Joyce family. It is easy to believe that a man who would see an innocent man hanged would threaten and cajole a young woman in order to elicit information, especially in light of her father's ongoing detention in Galway Jail. Did Brady use Mary to turn Mathias? Under Brady's questioning, did Mary reveal the identities of the killers she had seen commit the murders from her hilltop perch? Was that information then conveyed by telegram from Clonbur to the Galway City Jail where Mary's father sat in a cell because it was on the day after Mary's interview with Magistrate Brady that Mathias Kerrigan gave the government authorities the names of the killers of Joseph and John Huddy. Was all this a coincidence? *Or* had Mathias Kerrigan revealed the names of the murderers in order to protect his daughter and family from further interrogations and to put an end to his ordeal?

In a tortured statement from Crown Prosecutor James Murphy, Q. C., Murphy may have hinted at Mary's role:

> If the Virgin Mother of the God-born Child—if the parent of their own religion ever came in contact with them face to face, let them hope, for the sake of morality, for the sake of religion, and for the sake of humanity itself, that the family of the Kerrigans were at length—or rather at least *some member of them—* induced to reveal the terrible secret to which they were bound, and to detail the circumstances of the ghastly assassination they witnessed.

In his account of his role as Crown Prosecutor for the Huddy murders, George Bolton bragged that once he had extracted a confession from Mathias Kerrigan, he was able "to procure the evidence of other witnesses, who, when they found we were in possession of the facts, were afraid not to tell what they knew."

Royal Irish Constable Guarding a Police Hut

Again, according to her grandson, Mary Kerrigan was given two steamer tickets to leave Ireland, and Mary's future was placed in the hands of a matchmaker. The matchmaker knew of a young man, Michael Lydon, from Dooras, about ten miles to the southeast of

Upper Cloughbrack, who wanted to go to America and was in need of a ticket if not a wife. Dr. Lydon shared that "The marriage was agreed to on the spot, and they were married the very next day! As my grandfather used to describe it years later: 'No sooner said than done!'"

Dr. Lydon did not know who or what entity had provided the tickets for his grandparents, but in his memoirs, he emphasized how important it was that Mary get out of Ireland quickly despite the fact that the family had twenty-four-hour police protection as a police hut "sat in front of [Kerrigan's] door though there was another down the village [referred to as the "America" hut]." If Mary had revealed the name of the killers, then it is easy to understand why she needed to leave the area as soon as her departure could be arranged.

But Mary's role remains clouded by uncertainty. If, in fact, she did expose the three killers, then why wasn't she called as a Crown witness at the trials? A possible explanation is that the prosecutors for the Crown believed that the testimony of Mathias Kerrigan, the Hollerans, the Mannions, and Michael Moran, all men, was sufficient to see the three men hanged. It is all conjecture because Mary, the only person who knows what happened, died in 1928.[59]

* * *

In Upper Cloughbrack, as in most farming villages, the days were numbingly similar. The men arose with the dawn, did some work in the bog or fields, ate breakfast, tended their potato patches, repaired their thatched roofs, threshed oats, ate dinner, visited with neighbors, went to church, and slept. The women arose at the first hint of daylight and made breakfast for the men and children, usually a porridge known as stirabout, and served between 9:00 and 11:00. There was no bread to bake as there were no ovens—everything was done over an open fire. After breakfast, a pot of potatoes was put on the fire to feed the pigs.

---

[59] An interesting article about informer Michael Moran appeared in a 1904 syndicated interview of Bridgit Kerrigan, Mathias Kerrigan's widow: "[Mathias] Kerrigan has since gone to the bar of a higher tribunal than that of the Assize Court at Dublin, to answer for his share in the Mask mystery, while Moran, who had turned Queen's evidence, still lives under police protection on a small holding just outside America village." If, in 1904, twenty-two years after the murder, Moran was still receiving police protection, then the passage of time had proved insufficient to mend the wounds created by the Huddy murders.

The second meal was served around 5:00 and consisted mostly of potatoes, turnips, and onions, possibly with a protein of goose, chicken, pork, or milk in the potatoes. While they went about their work, the women were either pregnant or had recently given birth. The elders helped with the children as there was always a fire burning on the hearth and dangers in the barnyard, and infant and child mortality was high as evidenced by Cloughbrack's children's cemetery. Is it any wonder that no one would miss going to the fair or that patterns and pilgrimages were not hardships but something to look forward to and that wakes and funerals were viewed as festive occasions—a retreat from the monotony and grind of everyday life?

But in the early 1880s, there was a new source of excitement in the district: rallies hosted by the Land League. The *Connaught Telegraph* described the rally at Claremorris in County Mayo in April 1879:

> Since the days of Daniel O'Connell, a larger public demonstration has not been witnessed than that of Sunday last. About 1 o'clock the monster procession started from Claremorris, headed by several thousand men on foot—the men of each district wearing a laurel leaf or green ribbon in hat or coat to distinguish the several contingents. At 11 o'clock a monster contingent of tenant-farmers on horseback drew up in front of Hughes's hotel, showing discipline and order that a cavalry regiment might feel proud of. They were led on in sections, each having a marshal who kept his troops well in hand...and wearing green and gold sashes, led on their different sections, who rode two deep, occupying, at least, over an Irish mile of the road. Next followed a train of carriages, brakes, cars, etc. led on by the spirited hotel proprietor, driving a pair of rare black ponies to a phæton, taking Messrs. J. J. Louden and J. Daly. Next came Messrs. O'Connor, J. Ferguson, and Thomas Brennan, in a covered carriage, followed by at least 500 vehicles from the neighbouring towns. On passing through Ballindine, the sight was truly imposing, the endless train directing its course to Irishtown—a neat little hamlet on the boundaries of Mayo, Roscommon, and Galway.

Another giant rally had taken place in Clonbur on the day after the murder of Lord Mountmorres in 1880, and an energized crowd had greeted news of His Lordship's death with cheers.

Michael Flynn was known to attend Land League rallies where inspirational speakers preached opposition to the status quo. If Ireland were to be returned to the Irish, then everyone had a part to play. Was Flynn's role as a member of the Land League to punish bailiffs who evicted his neighbors? Flynn's last pronouncement was that he was going to his death for Ireland.

It is likely that Thomas Higgins also attended Land League meetings or, at the very least, was told what had happened at gatherings attended by the thousands. He was only twenty-five, recently married, and the father of a young child. His future was bound up with the success of the land movement.

Patrick Higgins's situation was different from that of Michael Flynn and Tom Higgins. He was three years in arrears on his rent, and he understood that when Joseph Huddy came into his yard it would be for the purpose of kicking him out of his home. The eviction notice, delivered in the cold of winter when there was no work to divert one's thoughts, could have been the proverbial straw.

Bailiffs have always had a difficult job, and at this time, it was a particularly dangerous occupation because they were regularly attacked and often travelled with police escort. The arrival of the bailiffs is vividly described by A. M. Sullivan in his *Atlas and Cyclopedia of Ireland 1900*:

> The advent of the sheriff and his posse of "peelers" [coppers] in the neighborhood was heralded by the ringing of the local chapel bell, and as at the whistle of Roderick Dhu [a Scottish chieftain], all his clansmen sprang from the heather, so in a twinkling all the "boys"—some of them of the mature age of sixty or seventy—and the dear girls swarmed to the rescue. And a rescue it very often proved, when it happened to be a seizure for rent. On such occasions, usually after the seizure had been effected, the crowd surrounded the bailiffs and police, badgered and worried them, drove the confiscated cow in one direction, and the sacrificial pigs in another, and crippled the well-meant efforts of the rent-raising expedition.

That is a benign version of the fate that often awaited bailiffs. Despite the dangers, Joseph Huddy, who was then in his seventies, loved his work. He relished evicting people and throwing them onto the road.

Huddy's enthusiasm for his job was known throughout the district, and it had cost his grandson his life. Is it any wonder that Michael Huddy, John Huddy's father, had refused to allow his son to be buried with the man who got him killed? (See Notes for Chapter 8 – Funeral of the Huddys.)

So, what actually happened on that winter's day in Joyce Country? A likely scenario is that Michael Flynn and Thomas Higgins, knowing that Joseph Huddy would be coming to Upper and Middle Cloughbrack to serve ejectment orders, planned the murder of Huddy on instructions of a secret ribbon society. It is probable that they did not know that Joseph would bring his grandson with him, but once the teenager appeared in the village with his grandfather, John was doomed.

As the Huddys went from farm to farm serving notices of ejectment, Tom Higgins and Michael Flynn followed the two men down the boreen to the home of Patrick Higgins. After serving Higgins, the Huddys went on to the Kerrigans' house to deliver the last of the processes for the village, unaware that their killers were right behind them.

In his despair, and with a copy of the order of ejectment in his pocket, did Patrick Higgins follow Michael and Tom into the Kerrigans' yard? In his frustration at the loss of his farm, did he take a stone from the boreen wall and at least attempt to strike Joe Huddy on the head? There was actually no physical evidence of a blow—only Bridgit and Mathias Kerrigan's testimony that the elder Huddy had been struck by Patrick Higgins. Was that act sufficient for Higgins to be charged with Joe Huddy's murder? The grand jury thought so, and a jury found him guilty of murder.

Another question: Did Michael Flynn, Tom Higgins, and Patrick Higgins rely on a conspiracy of silence from the people of Upper and Middle Cloughbrack to protect them? After all, during the nine months Kerrigan was in a jail in Galway City, the three men could have left their villages at any time and disappeared. Instead, they remained in their cottages, with their families, where the police found them in late September.

In a village as densely populated as Upper Cloughbrack, where people lived cheek by jowl and knew everyone else's business, it was inevitable that someone would talk due to petty squabbling or full-blown feuds. According to Kate Higgins's testimony, when she told her father about the bodies lying in the boreen, Patrick Higgins wondered if Kerrigan would try to place the blame on him. It is also known that at least two women had told the constables that they had seen the Huddys go into the Kerrigans' yard. And someone did reveal the location of the bodies in Lough Mask. Add a constant police presence to the dynamics of a crowded village, and it was inevitable that someone would talk.

If the murders were planned, and not the spur of the moment, the plan was poorly executed as the Huddys were killed at a time when the whole village was up and about eating breakfast or doing their morning chores. The people of Upper Cloughbrack would also have known that when the police were notified that the two men were missing, a search would be made, and such a search would lead to their doors. Even if the police failed to find the bodies, The Coercion Act gave them vast powers to interrogate and detain suspects.

After reading the differing accounts, it is my opinion that Mathias Kerrigan did not *willingly* participate in the murders of Joseph and John Huddy—that he and his family were bystanders drawn into the murders as witnesses. Unfortunately for the Kerrigans, because they were the last family to be served in Upper Cloughbrack, their yard became the killing zone.

The Kerrigans had known that Joseph Huddy was going to serve ejectment papers on them on January 3rd; William Burke, Ardilaun's agent, had personally given them the bad news. If it had been Kerrigan's intention to do away with Joseph Huddy, would he have murdered the man in his own yard in broad daylight with only his family to help in the cover-up? Patrick Mannion had testified that he had been drafted by Tom Higgins into assisting in the disposal of the body of the young Huddy, and it had been proved that Michael Flynn had carried the elder Huddy down the boreen in a creel. If Mathias Kerrigan had murdered the Huddys, then why was his teenage son the only Kerrigan to carry the bodies down the boreen? And why had Tom Higgins and Michael Flynn become involved in the disposal of the bodies of men they had not murdered?

There is nothing in newspaper reports of the trials to indicate that Kerrigan owned a gun (although it is likely that he did as it seems most men did own a firearm). The revolvers belonged to Tom Higgins and

Michael Flynn, and they had used them with premeditation to kill Joseph Huddy.[60]

After the trials, the Kerrigans were given police protection and housed in Galway City, but, eventually, the family returned to their home in Upper Cloughbrack. If Mathias had truly gotten away with murder, and innocent people had been hanged in his place, I do not think it would have been possible for the Kerrigans to have stayed in the village. Their neighbors across the boreen were the widow and orphans of Patrick Higgins, and Thomas Higgins left behind a toddler and a young wife—constant reminders of what had happened to their husband and father. Even so, someone did take a shot at Mathias the following year in Cong.

In his 1943 book, *The Corrib Country*, Richard Hayward wrote about the Huddy murders. His sources shared stories passed down to them during the ensuing sixty years, and most of it, utterly wrong, is as follows:

> The Huddy affair seems to be remembered in all its shocking circumstances as vividly as if it had only happened yesterday, and you would find it no great task to collect all the grim details from almost anybody within thirty miles of the place… Huddy's first call was on a tenant of the name of Kirregan [sic] of Derryclochbrack [sic], and at this place an angry mob gathered and literally pounded the inoffensive Huddy to death with sticks and stones. The grandson, running in terror from the dreadful sight, would have been spared, had not one of the men, realising that he would be an unfailing witness against them all, shot him in the back as he attempted to climb a wall… The upshot of the whole shocking affair was that Kirregan, virtual instigator of the crimes, turned informer…
>
> Lord Ardilaun arrived at the scene [of the dredging operation for the bodies of the Huddys] accompanied by the informer Kirregan, with whose help he was able to fire a rifle at the exact spot in the lake from which the dredger soon brought up the two bodies.

---

[60] Dr. Hegarty testified that he could not determine how many guns were used by the nature of the wounds, but seven shots were fired. What is the likelihood that one man emptied his revolver and then reloaded?

Many tales are told about Kirregan, who lived for years after under the rigid protection of the police, and the scene is still described when, for the first time after the executions, he arrived with his attendant guards to pay his rent at the Ashford estate office in Cong. It is recalled that Lord Ardilaun, who was standing in conversation with his agent, Mr. Jackson, turned to shake hands with Kirregan, but that on the informer's offering his hand to Jackson, that worthy, in spite of his Lordship's presence, lifted his stick and told him never to dare frequent the company of decent men.

True to its time, the hero of Hayward's retelling is expert shot Lord Ardilaun, and Kerrigan is the unredeemed scoundrel. But rarely do peasants write history.

In the 1901 census, Bridgit Kerrigan and two of her children, Martin and Bridgit, both unmarried, were living in the family home in Upper Cloughbrack. What happened to Matthew, the older son who carried the body of the young John Huddy, is not known, but family history has it that he immigrated to Australia. In 1883, Mary married Michael Lydon of Dooras, also in Joyce Country, and moved to Pennsylvania where they raised three children. Michael earned his living as a coal miner.

In 1904, a reporter then touring Ireland, wrote a syndicated article, riddled with errors, about the connection between the Irish town of America (Middle Cloughbrack) and the United States of America. Knowing of the Huddy murders, he stopped at the thatched cottage of Bridgit Kerrigan.

> Bridgit was placidly smoking a pipe, while the family pigs rooted and grunted contentedly in the yard...an old woman who was a passive participant in one of the most tragic of these dramas. In front of her dwelling two bailiffs were shot down and she mopped up the blood from the stones... Mrs. Kerrigan, although inclined to be garrulous in her old age, her mouth closes like a steel trap when any stranger broaches the subject of the double murder and neither bribery nor cajolery can induce her to speak of it.

It is easy to understand Bridgit's refusal to talk to the reporter about the murders. I doubt that even the passage of twenty-two years had healed that wound. In the 1901 and 1911 censuses, there are records for familiar names: Higgins, Macken, Mannion, Walsh, Coyne, Conroy, Holleran, and Kerrigan in Upper Cloughbrack. In the intervening years, did the murders become a part of their collective memory—something to be shared—or was it something that was so traumatic that the sooner it was forgotten the better?

In 1940, the Irish government resettled twenty-four families from Cornamona and Cloughbrack in Allenstown in County Meath, more than 120 miles away from friends, family, and the countryside that held the history of their clans.[61] Emigration claimed hundreds more. In Cloghbrack today, farms are scattered here and there, and, occasionally, an unroofed and crumbling cottage is seen along the road that replaced the boreen where the Huddys executed their last ejectment orders. Despite its location on the shores of Lough Mask, there is little activity as cars speed past on their way to Cong or Cornamona or Leenane. The only sounds are those of bleating sheep, carried on a constant wind. Although 135 years have passed since the Huddy murders, the postmistress of this tiny hamlet was familiar with the story of the murdered bailiff and his grandson. Even so, it is not Galway's most shameful chapter. That blemish is reserved for the Maamtrasna massacre.

---

[61] One of those moving to County Meath was Tom Mannion, the man who was told to get off the boreen by Thomas Higgins and, possibly, Michael Flynn. He died in Meath in 1943 at the age of ninety-two. More information on the Cloghbrack and Cornamona resettlements can be found at the *Connacht Tribune* at this link: http://www.mayonews.ie/features/22076-from-clonbur-to-meath-and-back-again.

Chapter 16
Aftermath – Maamtrasna

It has been called a murder;
It would more justly be described as a massacre.

Justice Barry on the opening of the Maamtrasna murder trials

On December 15, 1882, Patrick Joyce and Patrick Casey, the two men who were actually guilty of participating in the murders of the John Joyce family, and Myles Joyce, an innocent man who had been asleep in his bed, with his wife (who could not testify on his behalf), when the murders were committed, were "kicked into eternity" by executioner William Marwood. Oral tradition tells us that Barbara Lydon, Myles' widow, after giving birth to a daughter on the day of the execution, made her way to the Galway City Jail. "She positioned herself at the western end of the salmon weir bridge where she spent nine days keening her husband. From her ordeal, she developed a condition from which she suffered for the remainder of her short life." If you want happy endings, it is best not to read stories about Ireland.[62]

In an article entitled "Accusing Spirits" that appeared in the Parnellite newspaper, *United Ireland*, an angry William O'Brien (not the judge) wrote about Myles Joyce and all the innocents who had been executed throughout Ireland because "somebody must be hanged."

> Two of those men spoke from the Gallows with the noose around their necks. They were unquestioning Catholics. If the protestation on their lips were a lie, they knew they were stepping into an eternity of torment. The world's opinion was to

---

[62] Myles Joyce lived in the village of Cappanacreha, which, according to Father Waldron, translates to "the tillage plot of the cattle raid, plunder or foray."

them a feather's weight. The rustle of the Unseen was falling mysteriously on their ears.

Which are we to trust—the last words of man after man as he faces the All-seeing Judge or the verdicts of tribunals carefully concocted to convict murderers by hook or by crook? Better a garrulous peasant should be kicked into eternity by Mr. Marwood than the detective police should acknowledge itself baffled, and cream-faced loyalists go about in terror of their lives.

Both as to the tribunal and as to evidence, the proceedings against these men bear an indelible taint of foul play. Packed juries, bribed witnesses were the all-sufficient implements of justice. When the art of trying a man consists in picking out [from] the panel twelve of his deadliest enemies, verdicts of guilty and hangings may be had in any desired quantity.

All copies of the December 23rd edition of *United Ireland* in which "Accusing Spirits" appeared were ordered to be seized by the Government for containing matter inciting the commission of acts of violence and intimidation. O'Brien was ordered to appear before the Southern Police Court to answer for it.

In January 1883, Patrick Higgins, Thomas Higgins, and Michael Flynn were executed for the murders of Joseph and John Huddy at Galway Jail on the same scaffold that had been used to execute the three men convicted of the Maamtrasna murders. It would appear that with these executions a most violent chapter in the history of Galway had come to a close, but there was one last scene to be played.

On April 10, 1884, Tom Casey, one of the men who had turned informer in the Maamtrasna murder case, stood before the congregation of the parish of Tourmakeady, Galway, now a part of County Mayo, to make his confession before being confirmed by Archbishop John McEvilly of Tuam. With candle in hand, Casey admitted to perjuring himself at the Maamtrasna trials in order to save his own neck at the instigation of Crown Prosecutor George Bolton.

Response to Casey's revelation fell along partisan lines. Catholic Timothy Harrington, Member of Parliament for Westmeath, petitioned Spencer Cavendish, the Marquis of Hartington, acting for the Government, to open an inquiry into George Bolton and the

Maamtrasna murders.[63] However, the conservative press sensed that a conspiracy was afoot in the timing of the revelations. A week before Casey's confession, the newspapers had disclosed that George Bolton was guilty of gross immorality in that he had embezzled £60,000 of his wife's fortune. The press implied that in order to undermine the authority of the Government, it was necessary for those seeking justice for the men falsely convicted of the Joyce murders to vilify George Bolton who had served as prosecutor for the Crown. There was a sense of urgency to Harrington's request for an inquiry. In order to avoid the hangman's noose, four men had confessed to murders they had not committed. Their admissions of guilt had earned them the death penalty, but their sentences had been commuted to twenty years of hard labor. Although the Marquis of Hartington supported an inquiry, it was denied by Gladstone's Government.

Myles Joyce (Executed) and Informer Tom Casey

There was also the matter of the hanging of an innocent man. Myles Joyce, now viewed as an Irish martyr, was back in the news, and evidence clearly incriminating to George Bolton had been provided to Maurice Healy, an Irish nationalist politician and Member of Parliament. As Father Waldron notes in his book on the Maamtrasna massacre:

---

[63] Spencer Cavendish, the Marquis of Hartington, was the older brother of the assassinated Frederick Cavendish. He became the 8th Duke of Devonshire in 1891.

It appears that a barrister named Edward Ennis, a frequent visitor to Green St. Courthouse, one day succeeded in gaining entry to a room where Crown briefs were thrown after trials had ended. Natural curiosity impelled him to browse through them. There lay one of the briefs of the Maamtrasna Case. Even a cursory inspection suggested that it might furnish some judicial and political dynamite.

Ennis gave the brief to Tim Healy, M. P., a man who would certainly make maximum use of it. Healy…leafed through it. The handwriting, style, approach, showed that the Prosecuting Counsel, Peter O'Brien, Q. C. (afterwards Lord O'Brien, Chief Justice) had been the careless owner of the brief.[64]

O'Brien's annotations on the lists of names of prospective jurors for the trials in three columns was the identifying letter "C" for Catholic. In addition to this embarrassment were the never-mentioned statements of the young Patsy and Michael Joyce and the evidence of both Sergeant Johnston and John Collins. Healy found that none of the statements had been forwarded before the trial to the Counsel for the Defence.

In those statements was the damning evidence that the two boys clearly stated "the murderers wore bright clothes and had their faces blackened." The three Joyces [liars every one] had maintained that the murderers had "wore dark clothes and were not disguised." The point about the blackened faces was crucial. If they were disguised, how could the Joyce witnesses have recognized them? The case was totally reliant on direct visual identification of the murderers. The "blackened faces and bright clothes" would render this vital identification an absurd impossibility.

Harrington and Healy, along with a journalist from the *New York Times* and T. P. O'Connor, M. P., traveled to Maamtrasna, and, afterwards, published an article in *United Ireland* in which Healy accused Big John Casey of Bunachrick, among others, of the murders and dared him to prosecute the paper for libel. Casey did not, but George Bolton did sue for libel and won. However, as the *United Ireland* newspaper had

---

[64] Peter O'Brien, Q. C. was known as Peter "Packer" O'Brien for his ability to "pack" a jury with jurors who would favor the prosecution. This was usually achieved by challenging potential jurors of the Catholic faith.

no assets, he was unable to collect damages when William O'Brien, editor, declared bankruptcy. Lawyers for Bolton's estate also failed to recover damages as evidenced by notices in the *Times* of London.

Although an inquiry requested by Tim Harrington, M. P., was denied by Lord Lieutenant Spencer, Harrington, in a series of letters published in the *Freeman's Journal* (Galway), laid out the case against the Crown for the wrongful death of Myles Joyce. A booklet, published by Harrington, in which he summarized his case against George Bolton, R. M. Newton Brady, and Charles Barry, the judge who presided over the Maamtrasna murder cases, was widely circulated among members of Parliament. On October 24, 1884, Tim Harrington introduced a motion to debate the Maamtrasna murder case for the purpose of securing a full Government inquiry into this miscarriage of justice. Although, in the end, a full inquiry was denied, Harrington, through his motion, had succeeded in introducing into the Parliamentary minutes all the evidence he had gathered in favor of Tom Casey's confession, evidence detrimental to the Crown case. His efforts on behalf of the innocent can be found in Appendix B.

Despite Harrington's best efforts, in the end, little changed. One of the four men unjustly convicted of the crime died in prison and the other three, two brothers and a nephew of Myles Joyce, spent twenty years at hard labor for a crime they did not commit. When the men were at last released on September 24, 1902, they were put on a train from Dublin to Ballinrobe and walked the final eighteen miles to their homes in the Maamtrasna Mountains in the darkness and the rain.

Even though a formal inquiry did not go forward, there were consequences. The refusal of the liberal government to hold a public inquiry was among the reasons that Gladstone's Government fell in 1885. Because of the scandals surrounding George Bolton, he was dismissed from his posts. Although he was reinstated by John Poyntz Spencer in 1885 as State Solicitor for Tipperary, a state sinecure, yielding £450 per annum, was taken from him permanently, and he died with a tarnished reputation.

Today, in Britain, an effort is being led by Lord Alton and Lord Avebury to persuade the authorities to review the case of Myles Joyce, to declare him the victim of a miscarriage of justice, and to concede that he was falsely convicted and executed. In 2012, at Galway

Cathedral, a commemorative event was held on the 130th anniversary of Myles Joyce's death.

In the end, the question has to be asked: Had the years of continuous agitation accomplished anything in advancing the cause of Ireland for the Irish? I think that question can best be answered by Prime Minister William Ewart Gladstone: "As the man responsible more than any other for the [Land] Act of 1881—as the man whose duty it was to consider the questions day and night during nearly the whole of that session—I must record my firm opinion that it would not have become the law of the land if it had not been for the agitation with which Irish society was convulsed."

Epilogue

The Maamtrasna Murders bracketed nearly a century of violence. In 1798, Irish peasants had rebelled against their king. That uprising had resulted in the deaths of at least 20,000 Irishmen and led to the passage of the Act of Union of 1801 in which Ireland was forcefully absorbed into the United Kingdom. With the execution of the Phoenix Park assassins in May and June 1883, eighty-five years of almost constant agitation came to an end. Two years after Tom Casey's confession in 1884 in a Mayo church, the first Home Rule bill was introduced into Parliament but was voted down in the House of Commons. In 1893, a second Home Rule Bill passed the Commons but was rejected by the House of Lords. In 1913, a third Home Rule Bill met the same fate. Its defeat set the stage for the Easter Uprising of 1916 that eventually led to Ireland becoming a republic in 1949. It had taken a rebellion against the British Crown and a civil war to free Ireland from its tortured past.

Between 1883 and the Easter Rebellion of 1916, there was little violence in an Ireland exhausted from years of unrest. There were other reasons for the decline in agrarian violence. According to Laurence Marley in his biography of Michael Davitt, with the implementation of the Arrears Act, "The state paid £800,000 rent for 130,000 tenants who were now more concerned with having their claims heard in the land courts than…acting as part of the vanguard of the movement… The reality was that the Government's decision to address the issue of arrears seriously undermined agrarian militancy." Marley quoted author Joseph Lee in his *Modernization of Irish Society*: "The only social revolutionary policy that commanded widespread support…was peasant proprietorship, and the Arrears Act, by increasing security of tenure, took a significant step in that direction. The Arrears Act was the small farmers' charter."

Despite significant improvements as a result of the various land acts and rent abatement, there were still too many people living on land incapable of supporting them. The tenant farmer lived to extract not produce. Evictions continued apace. Bad weather, poor harvests, and hunger came again.

During the nineteenth century, emigration was a release valve for even greater unrest. In the 1850s, the decade after the Great Famine, one-million Irish left their homes, fleeing the greatest catastrophe ever to strike the island and its people. The population of Ireland in 1840 had been nearly seven million. In 1880, it was half that. After a decline in emigration during most of the 1870s, the numbers soared once again. When the totals for the 1880s are combined with the figures for the 1890s, it shows that another one million people left Ireland in the last two decades of the nineteenth century. In Galway alone, from 1871 to 1891, thirty-four thousand people emigrated.

From 1882 to 1885, ten-thousand of the West of Ireland's poorest took advantage of Tuke's Emigration Scheme and sailed to Quebec as part of an agreement with Canada to resettle farmers. Most moved on from the Canadian wilderness to America and settled in every city on the eastern seaboard, but a fair number moved inland to Pittsburgh, Cincinnati, and Chicago, or south to New Orleans. While many Tuke's passengers went back to their agricultural roots in Iowa's farm country, thousands settled in St. Paul, Minnesota, with the support of the Catholic Colonization Association directed by Bishop Ireland "whose parish priests go with the people and enter into their interests. Schools and chapels are opened at once, and strict rules are enforced against the sale of spirits." (More information on Tuke's Emigration Scheme may be found at minookamemories.blogspot.com.)

In the second half of the nineteenth century, America had become the world's preeminent industrial power, and it needed strong backs to work in its shipyards, mines, steel mills, iron works, and myriad other industries that produced the products that America and the world wanted to buy. The Irish, a largely rural people, who lacked the necessary financial resources to purchase farms, had moved into the heart of industrial America and took jobs in the most dangerous industries. In the hard-coal mines of eastern Pennsylvania, an average of three miners died every two days, but still they came. Although poor and uneducated, these jobs put real coins in their pockets—a novelty for most—and if they stayed out of the saloons, their children could attend school and move on to jobs where one might actually get to wear a white collar.

Although an ocean separated the Irish from their homeland, those left behind were not forgotten, and it was the hard-earned money of those who had emigrated that kept many of their relations on their farms or provided passage money for siblings to emigrate. And with new laws returning land to the Irish, and fewer people living on its acres, farmers had crops to sell at the country fairs with the money going in their pockets rather than that of a landlord.

A country that had once been severely over-populated now saw a drastic decrease in its population as immigration continued apace. In 1841, before the Great Hunger, Ireland's population was estimated at 6.73 million. In 2016, it was 4.76 million.

Joyce Country, the heart of County Galway, saw a mass migration to the coalfields and steel mills in Pennsylvania, Ohio, and Illinois. My great-grandfather, Thomas Lydon, a tenant of Lord Leitrim and Lord Ardilaun, left Glenlusk, Galway on Lough Corrib in 1876 for the coalfields of eastern Pennsylvania. In the 1880 census, he was illiterate, but he became the Treasurer for Lackawanna Township. He died in 1897 in a roof fall of coal in the Taylor shaft near Scranton, leaving seven orphans. His grandson, Paul Lydon, my father, graduated from the University of Scranton, the first in his family to go to college.

Mary Kerrigan, the daughter of Mathias Kerrigan, married Michael Lydon and moved to Lackawanna Township (Village of Minooka), a coal town on Scranton's southern border. She was illiterate and would remain so, and when she died in 1928, the whole of her life had been spent in grinding poverty. She did not speak a word of English and could neither read nor write, but her grandson, the late Dr. Joseph F. Lydon, became a cardiac surgeon at the Cleveland Clinic.

Another family who left Joyce Country for Minooka was the O'Neills. Michael "Squire" O'Neill immigrated to the United States in 1879. He later became the Justice of the Peace for the Village of Minooka, Lackawanna Township. His wife, Mary Joyce, and their four children left the Maam Valley in 1880.[65] Another eight children were

---

[65] A great-granddaughter of Mary Joyce told me that the first time Mary wore shoes was on her wedding day.

born in America. Four of the O'Neill sons went on to play professional baseball in the major leagues. John and Michael O'Neill formed the only Irish-speaking battery in Major League history, calling their unintelligible signals out in the open. Patrick O'Neill's career was cut short by an unfortunate encounter with a mule in the mines, but he managed the Minooka Blues, a premier minor-league team in the Catholic Temperance League. Younger son, Stephen Francis O'Neill, managed the Cleveland Indians, the Boston Red Sox, and the Philadelphia Phillies. As manager of the Detroit Tigers, Steve led the Tigers to their only World Series victory in 1945. When the playing field was leveled, the Irish prospered.

For many of the Irish who fled the hardscrabble farms of Galway for a new beginning in the United States in the years during and after the mini-famine, life in their adopted country was as difficult as it had been in Ireland, but there was hope that their sacrifice would improve the lives of their children or grandchildren. At the very least, for those who came in the last decades of the nineteenth century, there was justice in America. If charged with a crime, the accused stood before a jury of his peers—a jury drawn from those of varying economic backgrounds and faiths. That is not to say that there were not miscarriages of justice. There were. But in America, there was an appeals process that just might save an innocent man from the gallows.

Very few of those who came from Joyce Country to America returned to the land of their birth. In the coalfields of Pennsylvania, they had traded the green hills and mountains of their native Galway for soot-laden skies, and for the men, a life lived underground. The difference was that in America there was hope of a better future and that was reason enough to make America their home.

NOTES
Chapter 1
Vigilante Justice in Donegal

Plantation of Ulster: The Plantation of Ulster was the colonization of the Province of Ulster by people from Scotland and England during the reign of King James I. An estimated 500,000 acres, spanning six northern counties, were confiscated from Irish chieftains. Most of the plantation is now within the borders of Northern Ireland.

Bad Blood between the Earl of Carlisle and Lord Leitrim: According to "Surveying in Donegal," "Leitrim committed a greater offence when he deprive[d] her Majesty's representative of bed, board, and candle" during a progress by the Earl of Carlisle, Viceroy: When the earl arrived at Maam, he was refused entrance by the hotelkeeper, who produced a letter from the Earl of Leitrim justifying his actions: 'King, I will be obliged to you to fill the hotel with my tenants forthwith. Let every room be occupied immediately and continue to be occupied; and when so occupied you will refuse admittance to Lord Carlisle and his party. If there should be the slightest difficulty as to the filling the hotel, or the occupation of the rooms, my desire is that you will fill each with the workmen; but you must not admit Lord Carlisle... Any orders you may have received notwithstanding, I rely on you observing my wishes to the letter. – Leitrim.' As Her Majesty's representative in Ireland, the slight to the Viceroy had to be addressed, and Leitrim was removed from all public employments." ("Surveying in Donegal," St. Martin's-le-grande, Volume 1, *The Post Office Magazine,* October 1890-July 1891, W.P. Griffith & Sons, Limited, Prujean Square, Old Bailey, E.C.)

In addition to whisky and ale, the hotel sold cigars, tobacco, and oats for horses. It was also the location where tenants of Lord Leitrim went to pay their rents. (*Derry Journal*, October 28, 1863)

Philadelphia Fundraiser for Defendants: On June 2, 1878, "about 100 Irishmen, some of them evicted tenants at one time of the Leitrim estate, met to raise a fund for the defense of the men, McGranathan [sic] and Harity [sic], charged with the assassination of Lord Leitrim. 'We do not wish to countenance assassination, but we know that the men accused would not stain their hands with the blood even to rid the earth of a tyrant…' $150 were raised." "Fund for Lord Leitrim's Murderers," *Reading Times*, Reading, Pennsylvania, June 3, 1878.

Lord Leitrim's Successor: At the reading of the will, the 3rd Earl Leitrim's presumed heir, his nephew Robert Bermingham Clements (1847-1892), learned that he had been disinherited three years earlier because his uncle believed he would be an absentee landlord. "Leitrim also bypassed a brother and two sisters, and all of his property was left to a second cousin from Cavan, Colonel Henry Theophilus Clements. The colonel then made arrangements for the Donegal estates to be transferred to Robert Bermingham Clements, who had inherited the title of 4th Lord Leitrim. Despite the Algoe evictions and evictions throughout the Maam Valley in Galway, including a relation of the author, Robert was seen as a more caring landlord who brought in reforms on the 52,000-acre Donegal estate. In a complete reversal of the 3rd Earl's approach, the new landlord allowed evicted tenants to return to their farms and re-housed others. He also promised to provide a house in Milford to shelter the poor and destitute so that they could avoid entering the workhouse…

"In the following fourteen years, the 4th Earl of Leitrim initiated ventures to improve local business and built hotels and golf links to draw tourists. He also inaugurated a line of steamers to run between Mulroy Bay and Glasgow, via Derry, thus providing access to markets for the estate produce. On his death in 1892, he was buried near Mulroy amid signs of mourning from the tenantry among whom he had lived and for whose benefit he had worked." "Lord Belmont in Northern Ireland – Mulroy House." Blog. Web. July 26, 2015

A statue was erected to Robert Bermingham Clements' memory in Carrigart Square in Milford with the inscription, "He loved his people."

Chapter 2
Years Leading up to the
Formation of the Land League in 1879

Charles Trevelyan, Assistant Secretary to the British Treasury, the man responsible for Irish famine relief during the Great Famine, was an adherent of *laissez-faire* economics and a student of economist Thomas Malthus (1776-1834). He supported the Malthusian population theory that there are "checks" that keep population growth in line with food supply, such as famine and war.

Trevelyan believed the best approach to the Great Famine was non-interference and self-reliance, declaring that famine was a "mechanism for reducing surplus population" and "the direct stroke of an all-wise Providence in a manner as unexpected and as unthought-of as it is likely to be effectual." Trevelyan also wrote that the "real evil with which we have to contend is not the physical evil of the Famine, but the moral evil of the selfish, perverse and turbulent character of the [Irish] people."

John Mitchel, a member of Young Ireland, responded to Trevelyan: "The Almighty, indeed, sent the potato blight, but the English created the Famine." (Wikipedia: "Charles Trevelyan")

Chapter 3
Mini-Famine: 1877-79
A Turning Point

Potato Culture: Sir Walter Raleigh is credited with bringing the potato from the New World to Ireland in the late sixteenth century where it was cultivated on Raleigh's Cork estates. There is a record of cultivation in County Down in Northern Ireland as early as 1606.

The potato, if eaten in sufficient quantities, is a source of protein, amino acids, and important mineral elements including iron, calcium, and potassium, and it requires little preparation, minimal fertilizer, and very little land. Only one acre of land was required to support a family eating a diet consisting exclusively of potatoes. It was estimated that a barrel of potatoes containing 280 pounds for a family of five would last one week. Cultivation of the potato required only three months' work.

According to the Strokestown Famine Museum in Roscommon, the Irish supplemented their diet with "cresses, turnips, borage, nettles, frogs, hedgehogs and snails. Another common practice was the letting of cow's blood." The diet of people living in the coastal communities also included shellfish and vitamin-rich seaweed.

In the West and Southwest, ridges for potato beds ran uphill at forty-five-degree angles to provide enough food for the family. (On a cloudy day, the ridges are still visible.) As potato cultivation required little land to feed a family, young couples were able to marry and rear families on postage-sized lots. As a result, in the 1820s, Ireland's population exploded. The baby boom of the 1820s would have dire consequences for the Irish peasantry when the potato crop failed in 1845.

By the 1840s, the decade of the Great Famine, the potato was the staple food for the majority of the population, and more than two million acres were under cultivation. In 1845, the fungus that destroyed the potato crop made its first appearance in the South. Instead of a healthy potato, the people of Kerry and Cork found a rotting, putrid, black tuber. It was when the crop of 1846 failed utterly that the magnitude of the disaster became apparent.

Chapter 4
The Land League

The Land Act of 1881: From A. M. Sullivan, *Atlas and Cyclopedia of Ireland 1900*: "The main feature of the bill was the establishment of Land courts throughout the country to arbitrate between landlords and tenants, with power to adjudicate a scale of fair rents in all cases where lands were held by tenants-at-will… Though this bill was a wonderful advance on Mr. Gladstone's first concession in this direction in 1870, it had some serious defects rendering it almost useless to the majority of tenants who were in arrear for rent for two or three years."

The act, as amended, stated that the tenant should pay one-third the amount owed the landlord; that the Government should, out of the public treasury, pay one-third to the landlords; and that the landlords should forego the remaining one-third."

Chapter 5
The Land War (1879-1882)

Origin of the Term "Boycott": American Reporter, James Redpath, in his "Talks about Ireland," attributed the coining of the word "boycott" to Father John O'Malley of The Neale. Soon after the decree of ostracism was issued against Captain Boycott in late September 1880, while dining with the priest, Redpath stated that the term, "moral and social excommunication," then in use, would not serve their purposes. Father O'Malley thought a new word, named after the malevolent Captain

Boycott, *would* work. Although O'Malley coined the word, Redpath was responsible for "boycott" first appearing in print.

Ironically, Father O'Malley had promoted the idea of social ostracism as a way to avoid violence. Instead, the boycott became a way for tenants to punish and retaliate.

Parnell on Evictions: At an outdoor meeting, Parnell asked what one was to do with a tenant who bid on a farm taken from a neighbor who had been evicted. The crowd shouted: "Shoot him! Kill him." Parnell's response was: "I wish to point out a very much better way, a more Christian and charitable way, which will give the lost sinner an opportunity of repenting. When a man takes a farm from which another has been evicted, you must shun him on the roadside, you must shun him in the streets of town, you must shun him at the shop counter, you must shun him in the fair and in the marketplace, and even in the house of worship, by leaving him severely alone, by putting him into a moral Coventry, by isolating him from the rest of his kind as if he were a leper of old."

In framing the boycott, Parnell borrowed much of his speech from American reporter James Redpath, who had used similar language at a rally attended by two thousand in Ballintaffey, County Mayo, on September 15, 1880, four days prior to Parnell's speech.

Chapter 6
Murder of Lord Mountmorres
September 25, 1880

Lord Mountmorres's Body Conveyed to Dublin: "A considerable excitement was apparent on the part of two men who had driven the hearse and mourning coach employed to take the body and the mourners to Galway for conveyance to Dublin. These men were asked by one of the deceased's relatives to assist in placing the corpse in the coffin. Without the least reason being assigned, they flatly refused to do so... After much ado, the news correspondent and his driver laid the body in the coffin. From information received, it was thought wise that the corpse should not be taken through the place where the fair was being held. It was therefore suggested that another route should be pursued, but to this the drivers persistently objected... It was only on threats of personal violence from my driver [the *Times* correspondent] that they suggested a compromise, which would enable them to avoid the fair... Neither Lady Mountmorres nor the children left the house, but remained under the care of Lady Mountmorres's brother, Major Broadrick. At the gate leading from the park, Father Lavelle, the parish priest of Cong, who had been a personal friend of the deceased, and who last met him at a social party at Lord Ardilaun's, was present, the majority of them having gone to the fair." (*Times*, September 30, 1880)

The coffin of polished oak had on the breastplate the following: *William Browne de Montmorency, fifth Viscount Mountmorres. Born 21st of April 1832. Assassinated in the county of Galway, 25th of September 1880.*

Dr. John Hegarty – Dr. Hegarty, who was involved in nearly every murder in Joyce Country in the 1880s, graduated from Queen's College, Belfast in June 1872 and was a member of the Church of Ireland. With Lord Ardilaun's death in 1915, Ashford and various Galway estates were left to Arthur Guinness's brother, Viscount Iveagh, with the knowledge and permission of Ardilaun's wife. Two exceptions were made to that bequest. "One was to allow Lady Ardilaun to remove from Ashford House any property she may wish to have." The second exception was for Dr. Hegarty: "I except from the above-named bequest to my brother the house and lands held from me by Dr. Hegarty of Poliska, Clonbur." *Irish Times*, April 30, 1915

Threats to the Mountmorres Family: "The Hon. A.H.T. Montmorency, brother of the deceased, and a member of the medical profession, stated that the condition of things at Clonbur had been found by the family to amount to a reign of terror. The cook in his late brother's employment had to leave because of threats sent to her of personal violence should she continue in the service; how a boy in the family was never allowed to leave the house because of threats to take his life…; how it was impossible to obtain a messenger to convey telegrams to the nearest telegraph office, in consequence of which the members of the family had to go themselves." ("The Murder of Lord Mountmorres," *Times*, September 30, 1880)

Lord Mountmorres's widow found it necessary to have the police cut down trees for firewood as no one would cut the wood or sell it to her. Her Ladyship and her four orphans were boycotted so efficiently that the family returned to England. When Queen Victoria learned of her predicament, the family was provided with an apartment at Hampton Court. The former palace of Henry VIII and Anne Boleyn had been turned into apartments, some grand and some quite modest.

In March 1884, representatives of Lord Mountmorres were awarded £3,000 under the provisions of the Prevention of Crime (Ireland) Act. Up to June 30, 1888, £22,450 had been awarded by the Lord Lieutenant of Ireland to the personal representatives of persons killed and £20,185 to persons injured during the three years of the Land War. After Her Ladyship's departure, Ebor Hall was used to house fourteen constables who were there to suppress violence and ensure the peace.

In 1888, Lady Mountmorres appeared before the Parnell Commission: "All eyes were bent on the tall, pale, elegant, and sorrowful-looking lady, who ascended noiselessly into the witness-box. This was Lady Mountmorres, widow of the landlord who in September 1880, was murdered in Galway—still this county Galway of misery and crime. The lady testified that prior to 1879, and the rise of the Land League, 'There had been nothing but good feeling between her husband and tenants; how after that date, when the Land League meetings began, the tenants became rough and rude, and refused to pay rent; how her husband took out an ejectment notice against Sweeney; how a League meeting followed, and how the murder of her husband was perpetrated several weeks after the meeting.'

"When questioned by Charles Russell, Lady Mountmorres stated that she was unaware of any other reason for her husband's unpopularity. She did not know that his conduct at the Petty Sessions had provoked enmity nor did she know of disputes between him and his tenants regarding his refusal of a long-existing right-of-way across his estate. When Russell continued to press, Lady Mountmorres's head dropped; her eyes half-closed; she sank into her chair in a fainting condition," thus ended the questioning of Lady Mountmorres.

Patrick Sweeney: In June 1883, the *Guardian* (Manchester) reported that Sweeney had been taken into custody while trying to board a steamer in Queenstown (Cork City), bound for America, and was released the following month. This was probably a result of information provided by a tinker named Hynes. In October 1883, the *Morning News* (Belfast) reported that Hynes, who had told the police that he had witnessed the murder (including the presence of a "little boy sitting on the side car"), had provided the authorities with the names of the murderers. Although nothing came of the tinker's revelations, there is little doubt that Sweeney was re-interviewed as a result of Hynes's statement. Convinced of his complicity, the police continued to pursue Sweeney. A Sweeney descendant believes that Patrick died in Galway between 1901-04, but his son, another Patrick, immigrated to Pittsburgh.

Ebor Hall: On October 24, 1880, the *Tuam Herald* reported that "the personal effects of the late Lord Mountmorres, owing to the excited state of public feeling in the locality, had to be removed for sale to Tuam. They consisted of nine mountain bullocks, four ponies, a carriage, a phaeton, and some harness. The jaunting car which the murdered nobleman drove and the whip he used, as also the pony, are to be put under the hammer of the auctioneer.

In 1894, Ebor Hall was to be sold at public auction. The mansion was described as containing "four reception rooms, five bedrooms, bathroom and w.c. [water closet], kitchen, servants' rooms, laundry and cellar, garden and lawn, enclosed yard at rear (containing three-horse stables, coach-house, hayloft, and dairy). There is also a steward's house and farm buildings. About eighty acres are in the hands of tenants… The purchaser would have the exclusive rights netting salmon in Tumneenaun Bay, Lough Corrib, upon the rod and line for salmon and trout on the whole of the lake. Ebor Hall is situated one mile [sic] from Clonbur, post town, three miles from Cong telegraph station and six miles from Ballinrobe railway station on the Midland Great Western Railway." (*Guardian*, December 1, 1894) Today, Ebor Hall is a private residence.

A Tenant of Lord Mountmorres: The following story was told to James Redpath by Father Watt Conway: "Last winter [1879], I was sent to visit poor Mrs. Walsh, one of Mountmorres's tenants. I found her weakened by hunger. She lives in a wretched house. There was not a bit of furniture in the house, not a bit of fire on the hearth, and no bedding but a few dirty rags. The snow was falling as heavily inside the cabin as out." (*Inter Ocean* (Chicago), October 25, 1880)

Land League Meeting at Clonbur the Day after the Mountmorres Murder: Scheduled speaker, American James Redpath, suggested that the Clonbur Land League meeting be postponed. When his suggestion was rejected, he chose to use the venue to denounce the murder in front of "a people indifferent to it." Redpath insisted that the men who had slain Mountmorres did the Land League no favor: "Lord Mountmorres dead is a stronger ally than Lord Mountmorres living. The man or the men who slew him have not injured landlordism. They have injured the cause of the Irish tenantry—for although you are innocent, the landlords have the ear of the Castle and your defense will not be heard there... Napoleon said that in war a blunder is worse than a crime; and assassination is not only a crime, but a blunder."

Redpath described the scene at the Clonbur meeting where the platform was built against the walls of the old stone church: "Thousands of the small farmers, their wives, and children came to the little town to attend the land meeting. None of them knew about the murder until they arrived.... Here, I was brought face to face with a fact...that the long struggle against landlord oppressors was a civil war and the killing of a landlord was not a murder but a casualty, for doing which the perpetrator is no more guilty of murder than a soldier who slays one of the enemy in battle... Not one word of sympathy, not one word of exaltation, did I hear...at the news of the assassination of Lord Mountmorres... People heard the news, asked the particulars, and then talked of other topics as coolly and with as much indifference as if they had been told of the killing of a bullock. The nearest approach to a word of sympathy that I heard were the words: 'I don't believe he was killed by a tenant; sure, he had so little land and so few of them that he *wasn't worth killing* [as] he don't amount to much.'" ("Ireland's Misery," *Inter Ocean* (Chicago), October 25, 1880)

Coercion Bills: British historian Godfrey Locker-Lampson pointed out the carrot-and-stick approach of the Government: "One day a Coercion Bill, the next the Land Act, then another Coercion Bill followed by a further Land Act. Brute force and charlatan experiment vying with one another for supremacy... In this paternal manner had Ireland been governed by her rules. On these lines had they devoted their genius to secure the loyalty of four million Irish subjects." ("A Consideration of the State of Ireland in the Nineteenth Century," G. Locker-Lampson, Archibald Constable and Company, Ltd., London 1907)

Irish Peerage: According to the *St. Louis Post Dispatch*, "Mountmorres represents that impecunious class of nobles which have served to bring ridicule to the Irish peerage. They were the result of the easy way in which men were made Irish peers in the last [eighteenth] century." ("Lord Mountmorres, The Last Landlord Victim of Irish Vengeance and Spite," October 5, 1880)

Chapter 7
Arthur Guinness, 1ˢᵗ Baron Ardilaun

Lord Ardilaun – The "much loved" Lord Ardilaun's reputation took a hit with the arrest and prosecution in October 1881 of Father Watt Conway, a parish priest in Clonbur, who assaulted one of Lord Ardilaun's bailiffs when he was serving the priest with a writ of suit in connection with a dispute over a causeway. The priest was sentenced at the Cong Petty Sessions to two months' hard labor by Magistrate Major Traill. That decision resulted in Traill receiving death threats. It became necessary for the major to travel with bodyguards. He also carried a belt with two revolvers." (*Times* of London, October 7, 1881) The priest's sentence was reversed on appeal.

An Eviction of a Tenant of Lord Ardilaun: In January 1880, a woman named Noonan was sentenced to three months imprisonment in Castlebar Jail for throwing a can of boiling water at Lord Ardilaun's agent. The following year, in January 1881, three members of the same Noonan family—mother, son, and daughter—were arrested at Cong for taking forcible possession of the house from which they had been evicted. (*Times* of London, January 25, 1881.)

But that was not the end of the Noonan saga. At some point, the Noonans re-occupied the cottage, refusing to give in to Ardilaun and his agents. Unfortunately for the Noonans, Ardilaun did not give up, either. In September 1893, a Dr. Ambrose wrote to the Chief Secretary to the Lord Lieutenant of Ireland, asking whether he knew that "within the past month, a man named Deskin, a bailiff on the property of Lord Ardilaun, accompanied by other bailiffs, attacked the hut of evicted tenant Nicholas Noonan, near Ballinrobe, and forcibly ejected him and his family without any decree of ejectment or other process of law." When Noonan resisted, Deskin pointed a loaded revolver in Noonan's face and threatened "to blow his brains out." A Mr. J. Morley countered Dr. Ambrose by saying that the bailiff had acted on a previously issued decree and that Deskin had only drawn his weapon after "Noonan had stabbed one of the bailiff's assistants with a pitchfork and was about to make another attempt to stab." There would be no third re-occupation as the Noonan "hut was completely destroyed" by Ardilaun's men. ("An Irish Eviction," *Times* of London, September 5, 1893.

The No-Rent Manifesto – The Manifesto had minimal impact on events in Ireland as rents were paid twice a year on "gale days," that is, May 1st and November 1st, making it difficult to gauge any effect the manifesto had on landlord/tenant issues. Historians have determined that those who had the means to pay their rent did so because they were unsure of Land League support if they withheld rent, and it was they who faced eviction. As for the poorest Irish tenants, regardless of any declaration, they were unable to pay their rents due to a lack of funds.

Chapter 8
Murders of Joseph and John Huddy

Galway City Jail: Prisoner Peter Broderick of Athenry, Galway, who had been arrested for "inciting the boycott" in 1883, kept a diary of his imprisonment jail. In its pages, he recorded the overwhelming sense of isolation he experienced behind the jail's stone walls. He recorded the monotony of prison life, occasionally broken by factory whistles and the 6:00 a.m. church bell announcing the praying of the Angelus. Breakfast was a salty stirabout with coffee; dinner consisted of coarse bread and coffee. "Athenry Land League Part 2: Peter Broderick in Galway Jail," Athenry Local History, Ronan Killeen. Web.

The site of the Galway City Jail is now the car park for the cathedral.

James Hack Tuke's Comments on Huddy Murders: In his travels through the West of Ireland in 1884, Tuke's hired driver made the following comments about finding the Huddys' bodies: "'That's the point, yer honour, just past the schoolhouse…where they took them and put stones in the sacks, and rowing out past the big island they threw them into the lake just there between the big and the little islands. There is a deep hole near sixty feet deep, with an undercurrent, which they thought would suck them down and in, but they missed the hole by a few yards and they were found in only twenty feet of water.' It was all done in open daylight, and no doubt in the presence of nearly the whole village. Can you imagine a more ghastly savage picture of nineteenth-century society?"

Autopsy Findings for the Huddys: Dr. Hegarty and Dr. McGuire performed the post-mortem. "They found on examining Joseph Huddy's body a bullet wound in the middle of the forehead, about two inches above the level of the eyebrows. The bullet producing the wound penetrated the skull and anterior portion of the brain and was found lodged in the sphenoid bone. There was also a bullet wound on the back of the head, a little above the nape of the neck. Either of those wounds would be sufficient to cause instantaneous death." They found other wounds: a bullet wound on the left side of the head, about three inches above the lobe of the left ear. The bullet fractured the skull, but did not penetrate... A bullet wound was also found on the right side of the head, about four inches above the lobe of the right ear. They also found a bullet wound on the right shoulder.

On examining the body of the younger man, they found that one bullet had entered the back of the head and had lodged in the brain and another near the left parietal eminence. There were no contusions or marks of other injuries on either of the bodies.

Funeral of the Huddys and Compensation: "The funeral of the deceased was largely attended, there being a large number of relatives of the deceased in the neighbourhood, several of those resident on the townland of Cloughbrack being related to the deceased by marriage or otherwise. Both bodies were removed together from Clonbur for internment in the family burial ground at Ballinshalla. The cortege, however, had not proceeded far when, for some reason, the father of John Huddy refused to allow the remains of his son to be taken to Ballinshalla. The procession then split up into two sections: one following the remains of the old man to Ballinshalla, and the other those of the young man to the graveyard at Cong." ("The Lough Mask Tragedy," *Derry Journal*, February 3, 1882.

In December 1882, Thomas Huddy, son of Joseph Huddy, and Michael Huddy, father of John Huddy, sought compensation under Section 19 of the Prevention of Crimes Act, before J. A. Bryne, Q. C., Ballinrobe. At that time, Thomas stated that his father had earned £200 per annum as Lord Ardilaun's bailiff. In May 1883, Thomas was awarded £300, and Michael was awarded £200. (*Derry Journal*, May 28, 1883)

Chapter 9
Maamtrasna Massacre and the Phoenix Park Murders

Description of Maamtrasna: The mountains of Maamtrasna is a treeless landscape. The village is not so much "in" the mountains as "on" the mountain. A correspondent for the *Pittsburgh Post* described it as lying "in the wildest and loneliest district of the most remote regions of the Joyce country, Connemara, and is almost inaccessible, owing to the mountain fastness and miles of lake around which it is situated." The *Post* also reported that, at the time of the massacre, more than three years after the assassination of the 3rd Lord Leitrim, with few exceptions, no rent had been paid to George Robinson, agent for the 4th Lord Leitrim. ("The Joyce Murders," November 16, 1882)

Today, there is little evidence of the congested village of the 1880s. The terrain remains unchanged from the time of the massacre with sheep negotiating rocky ledges looking for edible grasses among the gorse and heather.

John Joyce's Farm: John had leased his farm from the infamous 3rd Lord Leitrim. After he was evicted in 1877, John, a widower, married Bridgit Casey O'Brien, a widow with four children, and moved to her farm in Maamtrasna.

Chapter 10
First Trial of Patrick Higgins

Packed Juries: In "Her Majesty's Most Gracious Speech," dated February 26, 1883, Mr. William O'Brien, a Member of Parliament from Cork (not to be confused with Justice William O'Brien), addressed the bias of juries in Ireland: "The fact that one Whig Catholic was retained on each jury only made the exclusion of his co-religionists more galling and [that the jurors chosen from] the panels prescribed by the Act were so concocted that those who would have heard the evidence free from vengefulness or panic were excluded, while those who were bidden to indulge their prejudice as a sacred duty to society were sworn." The City of Dublin had a ratio of Catholics to Protestants of five to one. Clearly that statistic was not reflected in the make-up of the juries.

Queen's Counsel or Q. C. – A Queen's Counsel is an eminent lawyer, usually a barrister, who is appointed by the queen to be one of "Her Majesty's Counsel learned in the law." As members wear silk robes, the award of Queen's Counsel is known as "taking silk." Appointments are made from within the legal profession on the basis of merit rather than a particular level of experience.

Police Huts: Police huts were described as tiny iron huts, iceboxes in winter and furnaces in summer. The iron floor, four inches above the ground, was covered with a couple of planks on which the constables slept. A newspaper report stated that "even if they were paradises of luxury, life within these huts must be an intolerable burden, so complete is the cordon of isolation which the country people have drawn around them, not a soul will speak to the occupants. They are avoided as lepers."

Chapter 12
Trial of Thomas Higgins

Gender Segregation: Haisa Diner notes in *Erin's Daughters in America*, "In Ireland, the separation of men and women in the home, the segregation of adults by gender in the family circle, almost universally characterized Irish family life. Irish men and women rarely ate together or sat together in their own homes. A temperance worker in the early twentieth century, trying to point out to a man in Cork that he was wasting too much money on alcohol, instead suggested that: [If you] 'put aside every day…a nice little sum, you could go somewhere with your wife and children for a real good holiday.' 'Go with my wife and children!' echoed the man in disgust. 'Sure I never yet walked the length of the street with them!' He spoke in much the same tone of indignation as if he had been asked to go for a walk with a domestic cat." (Johns Hopkins University Press, 1983)

Chapter 13
Trial of Michael Flynn

Michael Coyne, the Huddy Driver: A third account concerning the Huddys' driver comes from Sir Edward Fry's Memoir of James Hack Tuke in which Michael Coyne is not a man but a boy. Tuke had been traveling through Galway in May 1884 and had hired a jaunting car to tour areas impacted by the mini-famine:

"Our car-driver, who had been asked by Huddy [on the day of his murder] to drive him out from Cong, declined unless he would agree to take two policemen with him; this Huddy scorned to do, and induced another boy to drive. "And shure, if I'd gone with him, I'd be in the bag too, for I'd have gone to help him, shurely," said the driver, "but something told me not to go." There's the spot where the boy was told to wait with the car whilst the Huddys went up through the village to serve the notices. They arrived about nine in the morning, and the boy said he waited until four, and then, as no one came back, he drove home round another way. The police, hearing, asked him questions. He said he knew nothing, but he must have heard the shots and known something about it; but though often examined…the boy stuck to it that he knew nothing; but he got sick and pined, and was so bad that he got away at the last and went to America" [the United States].

A final account appeared in 1904 in an article that was widely syndicated in major American newspapers, including the *Saint Paul Globe* and the *Atlanta Constitution*. A correspondent, who visited "America" in Ireland, wrote the following about the Huddy murders: "Leaving the driver in charge of the conveyances, [the Huddys] finished the journey on foot. Only a few minutes had elapsed when the driver heard several pistol shots fired in quick succession. As the two bailiffs did not appear, he, after waiting some time, packed up his belongings and sought safety in the greater America on the other side of the Atlantic. The flight of the driver and the disappearance of the Huddys at once aroused the suspicions of the constabulary…" In his statement to the police, Coyne denied hearing shots fired.

Michael Flynn's Family: Bridget Higgins, sister of Thomas Higgins and witness Judy Higgins Holleran, was the wife of Michael Flynn. A few years after her husband's execution, in 1887, Bridget immigrated to the United States, settling in Minooka, Pennsylvania, south of Scranton, with her six sons and daughter Kate. It appears that only Kate and Michael, Jr. remained in Minooka. At least one of her sons moved to Youngstown, Ohio. Another Minooka resident, Mary Kerrigan Lydon, whose father had turned Queen's evidence against Flynn, also settled in Minooka, within easy walking distance of the Flynn family home. In such a small community, it was impossible for them not to have known of the other's existence as they attended the same church, St. Joseph's, and are buried in St. Joseph's Cemetery. In March 1911, Bridget Higgins Flynn, after visiting with friends across the Lackawanna River in Taylor, took shelter from the rain under a railroad car. When the train started to move, Bridget was killed in view of her grown daughter Kate, wife of Patrick Laffey, also residents of Minooka.

Appendix A
Maamtrasna Massacre

Maamtrasna's isolation in 1882 is best illustrated by the route Coroner George Cottingham took to get the murder site of the Joyce family. From Oughterard on Lough Corrib's western shore, Cottingham crossed the lake to Cornamona. He then went by sidecar to Cloughbrack. A second boat took him across a half-mile stretch of Upper Lough Mask. After that, it was uphill, on foot, and then down again into the village of Maamtrasna, a route taken by the many newspaper hounds who visited the murder site in the ensuing months.

In its remoteness, Maamtrasna developed its own system of justice, which might go some distance in explaining the barbaric murders of John Joyce and his family. Could the reason for this massacre be something as simple as stealing sheep or was it a combination of a number of things: Peggy Joyce's flirtation with police constables? Police visits to John Joyce's cottage? Another possibility was that John had helped himself to some of the dues from a secret-society fund. At such a distance in time, it is impossible to say with any certainty. But the lapse in years cannot erase the sheer savagery of these murders and the reactions of the people of the village to a horrific crime scene.

After finding John Joyce's body, John Collins went to the village for help. He returned to the Joyce home with many of the villagers. Several of the men went into the home where John, Bridgit, Margaret, and Peggy lay dead. Also in the house were Michael, fatally injured but still living, and Patsy, who recovered. While the villagers pondered their next step, the boys lay in the house, in the midst of the dead, unassisted and in agony.

Within hours, the hillside was peopled by villagers, a scene described by the *Daily Express* in its August 21, 1882 edition: "Dressed, as the females were in short red petticoats and shawls and sitting close together on the short grass of the upland, many of them smoking clay pipes, the sight presented a curious and novel one. Some of them wept loudly, others joined in moans of lamentations and a number gazed steadily at the house or watched with keen and cunning eyes the nimble movements of the constabulary." All that was missing was the popcorn.

Despite the crowd, at no time did any of the women offer to go into the house and care for the boys even when offered money by Resident Magistrate Brady. Finally, mercifully, the doctors placed Patsy Joyce on a pallet, and constables took the boy to Cong for medical treatment. He recovered and was called as a witness at the first trial but was quickly dismissed by the prosecution as someone who did not know his catechism and could not be relied upon to understand the sanctity of swearing an oath in court, even though his testimony would have saved Myles Joyce, and George Bolton knew it.[66]

According to Father Andrew Greely, in his book, *Irish Love*, "the Church didn't have much influence up above in Maamtrasna. In those days, the Irish-speaking folk had only a frail connection to Catholicism… They could no more grasp the rules of English civil society, so-called, than the people Stanley and Livingston met in Africa." In other words, theirs was a primitive society, isolated even by Irish standards, who made their own laws. It explains why John Casey of Bunachrick, who gave false testimony at the Maamtrasna trials, opted for silence over absolution.

In his account of the murders, Father Jarlath Waldron attributes their reaction to the dead and dying Joyces to superstition. "At the time there were frightening taboos about people who had died or were seriously injured outdoors. Not merely were the bodies not to be touched, but even the very stones on the road, fence, or field, on which they lay, were not to be moved." Apparently, those taboos came into play inside the Joyce home as well.

Surrounded by mountains, the people of Maamtrasna had learned to deal with the harsh realities of their existence by making their own laws and, quite possibly, acting as judge, jury, and executioner. Today, there is no evidence of the village, and access to the murder scene is left to experienced hikers, but the legend lives on.

---

[66] Patsy Joyce emigrated to the United States in 1896 through New York and lived for a time with his brother Martin in Cleveland. "Contact between the brothers was lost over the years when Martin returned to Ireland where he lived in Dublin and raised his own family." "Could you be related to the victims one of Ireland's most famous murder mysteries?" Ancient Order of Hibernians magazine, March 12, 2018

Appendix B
Maamtrasna Alliance

The Maamtrasna case was debated in Parliament and throughout Ireland and the English-speaking world. The refusal of the liberal Government to hold a public inquiry was among the reasons that Gladstone's Government fell in 1885. After its refusal, Irish members of Parliament, under the leadership of Charles Stewart Parnell, defected from Gladstone's Labour Party and supported the opposition Tories under the leadership of Randolph Churchill. That coalition became known as The Maamtrasna Alliance.

Member of Parliament for Westmeath, Timothy Harrington, took it upon himself to address the injustices of the Maamtrasna trials by publishing a pamphlet entitled "The Maamtrasna Massacres — Impeachment of the Trials." In the pamphlet, he dismantled the Government's case against the eight men accused of the deaths of the Joyce family and pointed the figure at the man most responsible for this miscarriage of justice and the death of the innocent Myles Joyce: George Bolton, Crown Prosecutor.

Impeachment of the Trials by Timothy Harrington, M. P.
Dublin National Office
70 Middle Abbey Street – 1884

Suppression of Evidence by the Crown

I am free to confess that when I entered upon the examination of this extraordinary case, though I was convinced of the perfect innocence of the poor man [Myles Joyce] who, standing on the scaffold, declared he knew nothing of the murder, I yet was willing to admit that Crown officials were deceived by the strange fabrication of the Joyces [the fabricating Joyces]. It may well alarm every honest man in Ireland, whatever may be his religious or political creed, when I assert that from official documents in the possession of the Crown, and by the handwriting of officials themselves, I shall be able to prove that not one, but the whole eight Maamtrasna prisoners were convicted of murder upon evidence which the very briefs in the hands of the Crown counsel showed to be false.

A copy has come into my hands of the brief made out for the prosecuting counsel in this case and bearing the name "George Bolton, Crown Solicitor" on the back, as well as the words, "Brief on behalf of the Crown." No less than four depositions in that brief state that the actual assassins had blackened faces; but though other depositions were given to counsel for the prisoners they got no copy of these, and not a suggestion or hint was allowed to be thrown out during the trial as to the disguises and the blackened faces.

John Collins, the first of the villagers who found the murdered family in the morning, was examined at the trial, and came off the table without either judge or jury or defending counsel suspecting that John Collins knew a fact which made the whole evidence of "independent witnesses" and approver a murderous concoction.

Were the Crown Counsel and Crown Solicitor equally ignorant of the fact? No, for in the briefs which they held in their hands was fully set forth John Collins' evidence at the inquest, in which the following passage occurs: "I then returned to the house of the deceased, John Joyce, and we then found John Joyce, Margaret Joyce, Sr., Margaret Joyce, Jr., and Bridget Joyce, all quite dead. We then saw Pat Joyce and Michael Joyce. They were in bed. We spoke to them. We asked them what happened to them. Michael Joyce then told us that he saw three men in the house. We then asked Michael Joyce if he knew the men. He said he did not know them as they had their faces dirty. I did not speak to Pat Joyce."

Constable Johnston was also examined at the trials in Dublin, and made depositions at the different magisterial investigations. He was allowed to make his depositions and give his evidence before the judge without a suggestion being made as to the blackened faces, and yet on the second page of the Crown brief is given his evidence at the inquest, the day after the murders in Maamtrasna, from which I quote the following passage:

> I went into the house. I saw John Joyce lying on the floor with his head towards the fire—lying on his face dead. I saw his wife, Bridget, in bed in the room, and the two sons, Michael and Pat, badly wounded—both able to speak. I asked Michael, through

Sub-constable Lenihan, who spoke Irish, what had happened to them last night. Michael Joyce said in reply that two or three men came into the room and shot him in bed, and that he saw one of the men take up something like a stick and strike his sister, and that he heard his grandmother screaming about the break of day. He said he got out of bed and came down to the kitchen for a drink, and said he saw his father lying on the kitchen floor. After getting the drink he returned to the bed in the kitchen where his stepmother was lying. She was then living. Before the men came into the room he heard shots. I asked Michael Joyce how many men did he see and if he knew them. He said no, that their faces were black, and that there were three or four men. I then asked Pat Joyce what happened to him last night, but got no reply. I then asked him did he know them, and he said no, that their faces were black. I asked him if they had a light, and he said yes, a piece of bog deal [a root from an ancient fir tree]. I found a bullet, which I produce, on the floor where John Joyce was lying.

One may ask in surprise whether it is possible in a Christian country that an officer of the law, who gave that evidence at the inquest on the murdered family, would be employed for weeks after in hunting up witnesses, preparing a case, collecting statements, all going to prove ten men guilty of a murder upon evidence which his own sworn testimony attests to be false? Yet this deposition stands in the Crown brief, and only a few pages later on came his deposition taken in presence of the prisoners, where all this fact is suppressed. It may not have been strictly legal to ask a question as to his conversation with the dying boy, but surely the fact remained the same, and if the omission of the question can be justified in the eye of the law, is there any justification before God for hurrying men to a murderer's grave upon testimony known to the prosecutors to be false?

But the Crown had evidence of a class which they could and were bound legally and morally to give with regard to this portion of the case. It was never mentioned during the trial that Michael Joyce, the boy who died, the young man I should say, for he was 17 years of age, made, on the day succeeding the murder, a dying deposition before Mr. Brady, R. M. The jury heard nothing of it; the judge, I presume, knew nothing of it; and the counsel for the defence certainly knew nothing of it. Yet here in the

Crown brief it stands, a record now of the innocence of the prisoners and the guilt of the prosecutors:

> Dying declaration of Michael Joyce, Maamtrasna, taken by A. N. Brady, R. M., on 18th August, 1882: "Two or three men came in. They had black on their faces. I did see my father and my brother killed. I am very sick. I cannot raise myself up. I was a little while in bed when they came. I was asleep when they came in. I heard the dog bark. My own dog. They said something to my father. I do not know what. I have no pain at all. I was at Mass yesterday at Finney. My name is Michael. John O'Brien told me not to tell and Michael Malley. It was last night when they told me not to tell. They swore me on a book (Irish idiom for extracting a promise) not to tell. It is John O'Brien of the Wood. I am sure of it. (Signed), A. Newton Brady, R.M.

But this is not all. We have stronger evidence still. I have already stated that Pat Joyce, the younger of the two boys, survived his injuries. The Crown paraded him on the witness chair at the trial, and here is how they jinked the trick, according to the *Freeman* report: "The little boy, Patrick Joyce, who had been beaten on the night of his father's murder, was next brought upon the table, but through the interpreter he stated he did not know his Catechism, nor was he aware what would happen him if he told a lie. Under these circumstances the Crown did not examine him."

Of course not. But this boy had been in the hands of the Crown officials for three months, and surely even George Bolton might have told him Hell was intended for the wicked. Can it be credited, that while this pretty farce was being played before the judge and special jury, the prosecuting counsel had in the brief which they held in their hands, a dying declaration made by this boy, also on the morning after the murder, stamping as perjury the evidence upon which they were proceeding to hang eight persons? Hidden away in the last page of the Crown brief, as if stowed out of sight, comes this truly remarkable deposition:

> Dying Declaration of Patrick Joyce, Maamtrasna, taken by A. N. Brady, R.M., at Maamtrasna, on 18th August, 1882: "I did not know anyone who came in. I would tell if I knew. Three men came in. It was near morning. I was long in bed. I think it was about one o'clock. I did not hear any shots. I was struck on the head. I don't know who struck me. They were 'married men' (grown-up men). They had soot on their faces. They had

whiskers. They had bog deal lights. They had a 'kippeen' [a short stick, a switch] each. They lit them inside in the house. I was asleep in the inside room when they came in. I got three strokes. They did not speak a word to me or to any one in the house. I think they had no coats but bawneens [a waistcoat with sleeves made from undyed wool]! They had three old hats. I believe I am dying. I might know them again." (Signed), A. Newton Brady, R. M.

This declaration was taken the day after the murder, and with a view to being used at the trial of any who might be accused of the murder. Lawyers will appreciate the legal force of the words, "I believe I am dying," introduced into it. Mr. Brady, R. M., did not think this boy too ignorant to make a dying declaration, but three months later he is found to have gone so far back in Christian knowledge while under George Bolton's moral care that he could not be sworn, "as he did not know what would happen him if he told a lie." That evidently is a question of dispute among the saintly theologians of the Castle.

But was it intended that this boy should be examined? After all, may not the Crown Counsel have acted in perfect good faith in producing him on the table? Alas! Again, this fatal Crown brief which strayed into my hands comes up in judgment. And, oh, what a terrible story does it reveal in a few words! This boy's dying declaration is, as I have said, stowed away in the back page of the printed Crown brief. The brief itself bears date "October, 1882," and so early as that, a fortnight at least before any trial came on, we find, printed in italics under this boy's declaration, the following direction from the Crown solicitor to the prosecuting counsel: (Patrick Joyce has recovered, but his evidence is worthless.) Now, then, we have the key to the farce that was played before the judge and jury in placing this boy on the table. "His evidence was worthless." So says the discriminating Bolton. We should all be anxious to know why, if Earl Spencer could only bring his conscience to allow him make inquiry. Perhaps Mr. George Bolton and Mr. Brady will again turn out a fresh memorandum to explain Perhaps Mr. Justice Johnson, then Attorney-General, can smooth the difficulty, or Mr. Justice Murphy, then prosecuting counsel, or Mr. Sergeant O'Brien, Q. C., then junior prosecuting counsel? [Murphy had been elevated to the bench after the Maamtrasna trials.]

I shall leave the public to make their comments. I freely confess I could not well trust myself to give expression to my feelings with regard to this feature of the case. In bringing these chapters to a conclusion, I think I may so far anticipate the verdict of my readers as to say that I have established my case. Let Earl Spencer refuse inquiry; let the judge who was entrapped into a wrongful sentence on a capital charge rest satisfied with what has taken place; let Mr. Bolton and Mr. Brady mutually acquit each other; the public are now in possession of the facts, and officials who would acquit themselves of the blood of the innocent will need to vindicate themselves. Inquiry was refused. It rests with those who demanded it to say whether the cry for inquiry should not now give way to one for prosecution.

Appendix C
Parnell Commission

In March 1887, the *Times* of London published a series of articles entitled "Parnellism and Crime," in which leaders of the Home Rule movement were accused of being complicit in the Phoenix Park murders. During the coverage of the murders, the *Times*, a pro-Tory newspaper, produced a number of facsimile letters, allegedly bearing the signature of Irish Member of Parliament, Charles Stewart Parnell, in which it appeared that Parnell had condoned the murders of the Chief Secretary to the Lord Lieutenant of Ireland and the Permanent Under-secretary. On April 18, 1887, the day of its publication, in a speech in the House of Commons, Parnell vehemently denied being the author of the letter, calling it "a villainous and barefaced forgery."

According to A. M. Sullivan, in his *Atlas and Cyclopedia of Ireland 1900*:

> Ireland's arch enemy, the London *Times*, did not miss the opportunity offered by the Phoenix Park tragedy to unmask its batteries of slander against its victim, and singled out the great national leader for special attack…, the purport of which was to show conclusively that Mr. Parnell, Michael Davitt, and all the prominent Nationalists were secretly in league with the Invincibles, the Moonlighters, and all the malcontents and miscreants of the period. Not only in league with the latter, but had instigated and abetted their evil deeds, especially the Phoenix Park murders. That money had been advanced from the Land League fund to James Carey, of the Invincibles, and others, to forward their nefarious designs, was also averred. No qualifying doubts or hesitancy characterized the language in which these serious charges against Parnell and his colleagues were set down; but, on the contrary, a solemn, portentous tone pervaded the writer's startling avowal.

The letters had been acquired by the *Times* from Richard Pigott, an Irish journalist, who had been paid £1,780 for the facsimiles. Pigott, who had once worked for the Land League in Ireland, left the League after accusing its treasurer, Michael Fagan, of being unable to account for £100,000 of its funds. As a result, from 1884 on, Pigott sold information to the League's political opponents in an effort to destroy Parnell's career.

In response to Parnell's denial of authorship, the British Government established a special commission, whose purpose was to investigate the charges made against Parnell and the Home Rule party. However, the Commission did not limit itself to the forgeries but also examined the violent aspects of the Land War.

Although the Irish Nationalist members of Parliament indicated that they were satisfied with the main result of the Commission, a modern reader might be less "satisfied" as the Irish witnesses were portrayed as buffoonish characters reminiscent of the anti-Irish cartoons published in America in the mid eighteenth century of simian-like creatures with big heads and small brains. Their speech was also mocked, but, apparently, the caricature failed to produce the result the opposition had hoped for, that is, evidence of Land League support for agrarian violence.

Once the scope of the inquiry was expanded to consider Land League activities, witnesses were called in connection with several murders, supposedly committed by members of the Land League, including that of Lord Mountmorres as well as the Huddys. These transcripts provided valuable historical material.

The Comission sat for 128 days, ending on November 22, 1889, and produced thirty-seven volumes in evidence. In the end, Pigott admitted the letters were forgeries and fled to Spain where he shot himself in a Madrid hotel room. Parnell sued the *Times* for libel, and the newspaper settled with him for £5,000, a considerable sum, as well as attorneys' fees. After the settlement, Parnell returned to Parliament a hero. It was to be the apogee of his career. With the revelation of Parnell's affair with Katherine Shea, the wife of Captain William Shea, Parnell's career began its downward spiral. He died two years later in 1891.

Appendix D
Lord Ardilaun after the
Lough Mask Murders

Throughout the years of the Land War, Lord Ardilaun remained at Ashford House, a witness to one of Ireland's most turbulent eras. But after six years of famine and unrest, Galway, now known as "A Murderer's Country" was exhausted, and both landlord and tenant wanted an end to the agitation and violence. Steps in that direction were taken with the implementation of the 1880 and 1881 land acts, but there was so much more to be done.

In 1885, the Purchase of Land Act (Ireland), commonly known as the Ashbourne Act, named after Edward Gibson, Lord Ashbourne, the Lord Chancellor of Ireland, was passed by the conservative Government of Lord Salisbury. The act set up a fund of £5 million for the purpose of funding tenant land purchases with a fixed interest rate of four percent. The act was passed to appease Charles Stewart Parnell, whose support Tory Prime Minister Salisbury needed in order to stay in power. The next year, in 1886, Lord Ardilaun became the first nobleman in Ireland to sell part of his acres to his tenants for the purpose of creating "peasant proprietors." The act was extended in 1889 with an additional £5 million added to the funds.

In November 1890, in a speech in the House of Lords, Lord Ardilaun denied that "Irish landlords intend to avail themselves of the policy of land purchase for the purpose of fleeing the country. Rather, he insisted that the overwhelming majority of Irish resident landlords wished to continue to live in Ireland, "their own country." However, he acknowledged that old grievances had made it difficult for landlord and tenant to come together, but he hoped that "every class may continue to live together in Ireland, but under happy conditions that shall be more permanent and happy."

By 1916, "final offers had been accepted from the Congested Districts' Board for over 2,000 acres of the Guinness estate in County

Mayo and for almost 28,000 acres in County Galway. The Board paid £50,000 for the Galway acreage… The Guinness family retained Ashford House and the surrounding woods until 1939, when the property was sold to the Irish Government."

When viewed as a man of his times, Lord Ardilaun rises above most of the large landowners in Ireland. Ardilaun did hire locally. He did attempt to educate his tenants' children. He did try to improve the living conditions of his tenants, and he did show restraint when pressing his tenants for back rent. He also sponsored the Dublin Artisan's Dwellings Company that built cottages for poor Dubliners at reasonable rents. On the other hand, he lived in a make-believe castle in the midst of a manufactured Camelot. Beyond the walls and gardens of Ashford House was grinding poverty and a peasantry subjected to the vicissitudes of life—most of them unpleasant.

Ardilaun's guests at Ashford House included the Prince of Wales, who came for the shooting.[67] His wife was Olivia Hedges-White, the daughter of the Earl of Bantry. Upon his father-in-law's death, Lord Ardilaun acted as trustee for the vast White properties in Counties Cork and Kerry. Ardilaun earned hostile press when, during the famine winter of 1897-98, he "pressed for arrears of rent. These arrears originally amounted to £23,000, and were bought by the trustees for £7,000. Having already collected £12,000, the trustees are now trying to extort the remainder."

There is no doubt that Lord Ardilaun loved Ireland. He donated to the City of Dublin the park that became known as St. Stephen's Green and provided £150,000 pounds for the restoration of the Church of Ireland's St. Patrick's Cathedral, Dublin, which begs the question: If Lord Ardilaun was able to donate such an incredibly large sum for the repair of a house of worship, why was he pressing impoverished tenants in Cork and Kerry for £11,000 in rent. It would appear that a love of Ireland did not necessarily translate to a love of the Irish.

---

[67] In 1904, a famine year in the West, the Prince of Wales altered his plans to go shooting at Ashford House. Instead, the gluttonous royal made a tour of Galway to comfort the hungry. "To Investigate Famine – Prince of Wales is Planning a Visit to the Emerald Isle," *Topeka Daily Capital*, December 2, 1904.

Appendix E
Connemara

Before Ireland's entry into the European Union, Connemara in the far west of County Galway, knew only unrelenting poverty. But the backdrop to so much misery is a land of nearly indescribable beauty, and it is best to leave the description of such a magnificent landscape to an Irish native. In 1909, Irish poet, Jane Barlow, published *Irish Ways*, a collection of stories about the lives of the Irish peasantry. Here are her descriptions of Connemara, its inhabitants and their customs:

Its wild west winds sweep into its vast-vaulted skies larger clouds and more fantastically piled up than are elsewhere adrift. They fling down portentously dark shadows over already scowling boglands; they let fall on clear-brimmed lakes many a slanted gleam of silver fire; the sunsets kindled among them are of an unsurpassable splendour. Hence all parts of Ireland, though especially the west and south, give much scope to the study of vapour in rapid motion, with its miracles of light and shade... ut only beneath changeful skies do their utmost charms appear. Then many a little glen may be seen as full of iridescent mist as if a whole rainbow had melted there.... Far across the sombre floor of the bog a mountain range will hold stains of deepest pansy-purple in its hollows, and lift up peaks dipped in wild hyacinth blue; on hills somewhat nearer, the burning gold of gorse blossom, and dim pallor of ling, and smouldering ruddiness of heather, mingle themselves into one apricot-coloured glow under the sun. Close at hand, wide moss-green and apple-green slopes suddenly glitter all over with a network of crystal rivulets... Everywhere, spread abroad in unstinted measure by the acre or even the mile, lie the vivid hues that are prized when doled out thriftily in precious stones, and flower-petals, and fragile wings; and everywhere their brightness is enhanced by quickly recurrent gleams and glooms as the clouds pass floating double...

The people were on their way to a fair..., and we can indeed hardly overestimate the blank that would be left in the people's lives if from them were subtracted the fair-days and market-days which are so large a factor in the sum of their business and pleasure. We can imagine some future time when Irish peasants may adopt more strictly scientific methods of buying and selling, and dispose of their farm produce and purchase their household requisites at fixed prices in a great co-operative store, without any of the haggling and chaffering which is now an indispensable part of such transactions, and a source of agreeable interest to many onlookers not at all personally concerned.

"As a rule, friendliness prevails; while herds of cattle poking their foolish horned heads into the most inconvenient places; drovers shouting and flourishing sticks; flocks of sheep trotting along in a compact formation enforced by sagacious collies; pigs and calves plunging hither and thither, or mounted on carts behind the wooden bars of tall cage-like creels; horses and ponies exhibiting their best paces before studiously disparaging critics; small droves of dark turf-coloured donkeys, the property, most likely, of wandering tinker-people, acquired by means best known to themselves; hand-barrows piled with crockery, boots, tinware, and vegetables; market-women with baskets of fowl and eggs; stalls hung with garments, chiefly second-hand; tables covered with fruit and confectionery—all these things, accompanied by the strains of two or three fiddlers and pipers, make up a scene which has continually repeated itself time out of mind...

"It would be impossible to spend much time in rural Ireland without recognising the importance of "jaunting-cars," more especially in their humbler form, that most commonly seen. Though they are all built upon the same general lines..., none is more modifiable by cushions, springs, and tyres; none responds more sensitively to the asperities and amenities of the surface over which it rolls, or to the peculiar paces of the beast by which it is drawn. A drive along deep-rutted boreens, perched on a high, ill-balanced, unpadded seat, with unequal, iron-shod wheels, and a lolloping horse, prone to stumble, if not come down outright, is an experience that might well remind sporting people of a stiff run across country.

"Not only do occasions such as funerals, weddings, and fairs tax its capacity to the uttermost, but daily emergencies make incessant demands upon it. In fact, what with 'the loan of a lift' recurrent on the way, and the doing of commissions for stay-at-home neighbours, a car, however moderately laden at the outset, seldom reaches its journey's end with an unoccupied cranny to spare. All sorts of things hitch themselves on to it as it proceeds. A firkin of butter and a spinning-wheel may be sitting waiting for it at some wild, heathery-bordered cross-roads; and a bit farther on it may pick up under a hedge a rush-cased salmon and a couple of equally silent geese, or perhaps an old woman with some less fortunate fowl squawking and fluttering beneath her cloak.

"A 'burying,' for instance, with its accompanying 'wake,' is often for most of those who attend it an enjoyable social gathering, at which extremely lavish hospitality will be shown. This is a sign of the national propensity for laying an exaggerated and ghoulish emphasis on funereal affairs... And there are dances for the soon-dark winter nights, when the fiddle quits its hook on the wall; hurley and football matches; patterns and stations; hunting and horse-races, with not a little gambling and drinking, in response to the ever-effective demand for excitement by any means good or bad...

"Turf and the bog whence it came—they seem essential features in Irish country life, which failing them could hardly be carried on at all. Indeed, where would we be without our bit of good turf? is a question common among the peasantry. Happily the speculation has no very practical bearings, since nearly three million acres of turf beds, averaging twenty feet in thickness, may well be considered to leave little room for fear that supplies will run short... Living on the edge of a bog is in many ways like living on the shore of the sea... Also like the sea, bogs have their tales of perils and sorrows. Ever and anon, half a mile or so of one will begin to move...amid shrieks and groans weirder than the sounds made by breaking ice-fields... Open-mouthed bog-holes, murky and steep-walled, do not lack opportunities for gulping down bodily the benighted passer-by.

"Despite all disasters and mischances, it must be admitted that bogs have a charm of their own... Their sad-coloured mantle is here and there resplendent with fiery gold of furze and paler gold of broom, silver white of tall ox-eye daisies, and crimson and purple of loosestrife and heather. On a closer view it is seen to be embroidered with diminutive blossoms and berries that glow like jewels... Even the grey boulders among the gorse bushes are encrusted with scarlet-cupped lichen. They are haunted by flocks of wild birds, amongst which the snowy gulls shine conspicuously... And all these things are over and above the long-shaped turf-sods, which play so indispensable a part in Irish rural life that we can hardly dissociate it from the odour of the transparent blue smoke.

Biographies

Bolton, George – Crown Prosecutor in the Huddy and Maamtrasna murder cases. His interrogation techniques yielded results if not justice. His deliberate suppression of evidence, evidence that would have acquitted several of those charged with the murders in the Maamtrasna Massacre case, triggered a series of articles written by Tim Harrington for the purpose of exonerating those falsely accused of the murders, and in the case of Myles Joyce, his wrongful execution. Bolton's reputation suffered a near fatal blow when it was discovered that he had embezzled £60,000 of his wife's fortune.

Boycott, Captain Hugh Cunningham (1832-1897) – Captain Boycott, a former English soldier, was appointed agent by Lord Erne for his County Mayo estates in 1873. He became the first victim of the total shunning of those who assisted in the evictions of Irish tenants, a tactic that bears his name. When it became too dangerous for him to harvest his crops, he fought back by enlisting the aid of 1,000 Orange Ulsterman, but 1,000 troops were needed in order to protect them from local agitators. It was said that the Government  spent £10,000 on their efforts, or in the words of Charles Stewart Parnell, "one shilling for every turnip dug from Boycott's land." In a letter to Prime Minister Gladstone requesting compensation, Boycott estimated that he had lost £6,000 of his investment in his estate.

Brady, Andrew Newton – Resident Magistrate who investigated the Huddy murders as well as the Maamtrasna Massacre. Brady was aware of the suppression of evidence in the Maamtrasna case that would have acquitted those falsely charged with the murder of the Joyce family. He was awarded a knighthood and died on March 20, 1918.

Casey, John (aka "Big John Casey of Bunachrick") – Big John Casey, one of the killers of the Joyce family, continued to live in Maamtrasna with his son John, another killer, until their relationship deteriorated to the point where the son moved out of the house and "lived out his days nearby in abject poverty." According to Father Waldron, Casey's neighbors "knew about their participation in the murders, but there were some who sympathized with Big John's dilemma about his nuisance neighbor, if not his solution." (*Maamtrasna*, p. 315). In the 1911 census for Maamtrasna, John Casey, whose age is listed as 74, was living alone in his cottage in the shadow of the Maamtrasna Mountains.

Clements, William Sydney, 3rd Earl of Leitrim (1806-1878) –William Sydney Clements was born in Dublin in 1806. He chose the army as a profession, and after graduating from Sandhurst, he was commissioned an ensign. In 1831, he was promoted to captain and appointed to serve as an aide-de-camp to the Lord Lieutenant of Ireland. Upon his father's death in 1854, Clements succeeded to the title as the 3rd Earl of Leitrim. On April 2, 1878, he was assassinated near Milford by three assassins. He is buried in St. Michan's Church, Dublin.

Daly, James (1838 County Mayo – 1911 Castlebar, County Mayo) – The all but forgotten co-founder of the Land League with Michael Davitt. In February 1876, together with Alfred O'Hea, he purchased the *Mayo Telegraph*, renamed the *Connaught Telegraph*, an important instrument in advancing the goals of the Land League and tenants' rights. Uncomfortable with the direction of the movement, he resigned from the Land League and returned to local politics. He sold the *Telegraph* in 1888 and became a full-time farmer. (Compiled from Wikipedia: "James Daly")

Davitt, Michael (1846-1899) – Michael Davitt was born in Straide, County Mayo, Ireland in May 1846. In 1850, after being evicted from their farm, the Davitts moved to East Lancashire in England. The family lived in a poor Irish immigrant community with strong nationalist tendencies and a deep hatred of landlordism.

At nine, Davitt went to work as a laborer in a cotton mill where his right arm became entangled in a spinning machine, requiring amputation. After the accident, a local benefactor helped to send him to a Methodist school where he proved to be a natural scholar. It was during this time that he became steeped in Irish history and current events in Ireland and became radicalized.

In 1865, Davitt joined the Irish Republican Brotherhood (IRB), which had strong support among working-class Irish emigrants, and became the organizing secretary for Northern England and Scotland, in which he arranged for arms to be smuggled into Ireland. Davitt was arrested in London's Paddington Station on May 14, 1870 while awaiting a delivery of arms. He was convicted of felony treason and sentenced to fifteen years of penal servitude in Dartmoor Prison in Devon where he was kept in solitary confinement.  Due to public furor over his treatment, and after having served seven and one-half years of his sentence, Davitt was released (along with other political prisoners) on December 19, 1877, on a ticket of leave (parole). Upon landing in Ireland, he and the other prisoners were given a heroes' welcome.

Davitt became a member of the IRB's Supreme Council. Despite the enactment of the reform Land Act of 1870, he believed that the only way the Irish could improve their lot was by getting rid of landlordism and replacing it with local ownership.

On 16 August 1879, the Land League of Mayo was formally founded in Castlebar, Mayo. Parnell was made its president and Davitt one of its secretaries. The League pursued a policy of the "Three Fs" (Fair Rent, Fixity of Tenure, and Free Sale). Part of their plan called for an organized resistance to evictions and insistence on reductions in rents. Davitt's support of the Irish National League earned him a final spell in prison in 1883.

In the general election of 1895, Davitt stood for election in South Mayo and endorsed Gladstone's Second Home Rule Bill. In October 1899, he resigned from the Commons and became a lecturer on humanitarian issues throughout the world.

Davitt died in Dublin on May 30, 1906 from blood poisoning. The Earl of Aberdeen, then Lord Lieutenant of Ireland, attended his funeral. Davitt's body was brought to the Carmelite Friary in Clarendon Street, Dublin where more than 20,000 people filed past his coffin. He is buried in the grounds of Straide Abbey at Straide, County Mayo. (Compiled from Wikipedia: "Michael Davitt")

Ford, Patrick – Influential owner of the Boston-based *Irish World* that raised more than $100,000 in small donations for Land League activities in Ireland. Gladstone stated that "without the *Irish World* and the money it collected, there would have been no agitation in Ireland."

Forster, William Edward (1818-1886) – Forster was born to Quaker parents in Dorset in 1818. In 1846–47, he accompanied his father to Connemara, Ireland for the purpose of distributing relief supplied by the Society of Friends during the Great Famine. In 1859, he first entered the House of Commons as a member of the Liberal Party. In 1880, Forster was named Chief Secretary for Ireland and carried the Compensation for Disturbance bill through the Commons, a bill which was thrown out in the House of Lords. On 24 January 1881, he introduced a Coercion Bill in the House of Commons to deal with agrarian arrest that he believed was a direct result of Land League activities. He resigned from his position as Chief Secretary in protest of the Kilmainham Treaty that freed Parnell from jail. His successor, Frederick Cavendish, was assassinated. Forster died on the eve of a vote on the Home Rule bill, which he opposed. (Compiled from *Spartacus Educational*. Blog. Web: William Edward Foster)

Flynn, Michael – Convicted of the murder of Joseph and John Huddy. It is believed he belonged to a secret society that ordered the murders. He was hanged in Galway City Jail on January 17, 1883, leaving behind his wife, mother, and seven orphans.

Gladstone, William Ewart (1809-1898) – William Ewart Gladstone was born in Liverpool to Sir John Gladstone, a merchant, and Anne MacKenzie Robertson in 1809. He attended Eton and Christ Church, Oxford, where he had a double first in Classics and Mathematics and served as president of the Oxford Union Debating Society. Gladstone first entered Parliament in 1832 and served in the cabinet of Sir Robert Peel.

Gladstone's first ministry as Prime Minister (1868-1874) saw the disestablishment of the Church of England and the introduction of secret voting. During his second ministry (1880-1885), Parliament enacted the Irish Coercion Act of 1881, an act that allowed the Lord Lieutenant of Ireland to detain people indefinitely. He also passed the Second Land Act of 1881 giving Irish tenants the "3Fs". In his third premiership (1886), Gladstone proposed home rule for the Irish, but the bill was defeated in the House of Commons. Home rule split the Liberal Party and kept the Liberals out of office for nearly twenty years. In 1892, at the age of 82,

Gladstone formed his last government. The Second Irish Home Rule Bill passed the Commons but was defeated in the Lords in 1893. Gladstone resigned in March 1894 and left Parliament in 1895. He died three years later, aged 88. (Compiled from Wikipedia: "William Ewart Gladstone")

Guinness, Arthur, 1st Lord Ardilaun (1840-1915) – An heir to the Guinness brewery fortune. Arthur was born on November 1, 1840 at St Anne's, Raheny, near Dublin, and educated at Eton in England and Trinity College in Dublin. With his father's death in 1868, he succeeded to the title of 2nd Baronet. He served as a conservative member of Parliament, representing the City of Dublin, and was a supporter of Benjamin Disraeli's "constructive unionism," a belief that the union between Ireland and Britain should be more beneficial to the people of Ireland after centuries of difficulties.

Arthur was the first landlord to sell property to his former tenants under provisions of the Congested Districts Board. He died on January 20, 1915 at his home in Raheny and was buried at All Saints Church, Raheny.

Harrington, Timothy (1851 County Cork – 1910) was an Irish journalist, barrister, nationalist politician and member of parliament. He also served as Lord Mayor of Dublin from 1901-04. Educated at Catholic University and Trinity College, Dublin, he was the owner of *United Ireland*, an important newspaper in promoting Land League goals. In 1884, Harrington published a pamphlet, "Maamtrasna Massacres - Impeachment of the Trials," in which he dismantled the Crown Prosecution's case against the eight men convicted of the murders of the Joyce family and provided sufficient evidence that Crown Prosecutor George Bolton had deliberately suppressed evidence that would have acquitted Myles Joyce, who was hanged, and four men who were sentenced to twenty years of penal servitude. He served as Charles Russell's junior during the Parnell Commission hearings. (Compiled from Wikipedia: "Timothy Harrington")

Higgins, Patrick – Convicted of the murders of process-servers Joseph and John Huddy. He was hung in Galway City Jail on January 15, 1883.

Higgins, Thomas - Convicted of the murders of process-servers Joseph and John Huddy. He was hung in Galway City Jail on January 17, 1883.

Huddy, Joseph and John – Process servers for Lord Ardilaun who were killed on January 3, 1882 in Upper Cloughbrack, Galway, their bodies dumped in Lough Mask. Three men, Patrick Higgins, Thomas Higgins, and Michael Flynn, were executed for the murders.

Heraghty, Michael, Tullyconnell – One of Lord Leitrim's assassins who owned the gun used to kill Leitrim. He died in Lifford Jail of typhus while awaiting trial.

Joyce, Myles, 45, Cappanacreha, County Mayo) – In the heavily congested area of Maamtrasna, feuds were the norm as farmers fought over access to "sweet" grass in the uplands as well as animal trespass and sheep rustling, and Myles Joyce ran afoul of Big John Casey of Bunachrick. Casey's revenge was to implicate him in the Joyce murders. Myles was found guilty in the Green Street Courthouse in Dublin and was hung in Galway City Jail on December 15, 1882. From the time of his execution, efforts were ongoing in an attempt to clear Myles's name and vacate the conviction. In April 2018, Irish President Michael D. Higgins granted a posthumous pardon to Myles Joyce. After the Irish pardon was granted, Myles' descendants called on the British government to dismiss the case. More than one-hundred years after the murders, a marker was placed on the graves of the victims.

Kearney, Patrick – Publican in Clonbur who hosted meetings of a secret society in his publichouse and back garden. It is believed that the murder of Lord Mountmorres was planned at Kearney's pub and that he recruited the men who assassinated the viscount.

Kerrigan, Mathias – Process servers Joseph and John Huddy were murdered in his yard while serving ejectment decrees in Upper Cloughbrack, Galway. He was detained without charge for nine months before turning informer. It was his testimony that convicted Patrick Higgins, Thomas Higgins, and Michael Flynn of the Huddy murders. He died in 1898.

McElwee, Michael, Ballywhoriskey, a tailor – One of Lord Leitrim's assassins who died of a fever before being implicated in the murder. His father's eviction the previous year may have been the motive for his participation in the murder. According to the *Guardian*: "The only bidders [at auction] for the farm were M'Elwaine's [sic] son and Lord Leitrim himself, and Lord Leitrim became the purchaser for a sum equal to 108 years' purchase of the rent. M'Elwaine managed to retain possession of the house till long after the sale, and was dispossessed with difficulty…" "An Irish Agrarian Dispute," *Guardian*, November 13, 1878. McElwee's eviction is an indication of the lengths Leitrim would go to in order to evict an unwanted tenant.

McGranaghan, Bernard, James and Thomas McGranaghan – Three brothers arrested in connection with the assassination of Lord Leitrim. Although they were held for months in Lifford Jail, they were never tried for Leitrim's murder.

Mountmorres, Lord (1832-1880) – William Browne de Montmorency was born in Ireland and educated at Trinity College, Dublin. He used his wife's dowry to purchase Ebor Hall on Loch Corrib in Galway. He served as a magistrate at the petty sessions and was assassinated on September 25, 1880 by members of a secret ribbon society as it was believed that he was in the pay of Dublin Castle.

Mountmorres's funeral service was held at Monkstown Church and was conducted by the Rev. Gilbert Mahaffy, who stated that he believed that the murder was not against Mountmorres personally but against people of his class. (He was wrong.) Mountmorres is buried in the family plot in the Monkstown graveyard in South Dublin.

O'Brien, Justice William (1832-1899) was born in County Cork and was admitted to the Irish bar in 1855, becoming Queen's Counsel in 1872. He was appointed a judge of the High Court of Justice in Ireland in 1882, the year of the Huddy and Phoenix Park murder trials. Even a glowing obituary in the *Law Times* admitted that he had not been highly thought of as a barrister, and it was believed that he owed his appointment to the influence of his friend, the Lord Chancellor of Ireland, Sir Edward Sullivan. The politically charged atmosphere of the Phoenix Park trials, over which he presided, required police protection until his death in December 1899. (Wikipedia: "William O'Brien")

Parnell, Charles Stewart – Charles Stewart Parnell was born in 1846 in County Wicklow to John Henry Parnell, a wealthy Anglo-Irish landowner, and his American wife, Delia Tudor Stewart. Although Parnell studied at Cambridge, he never completed his degree. Parnell was first elected to the House of Commons as a Home Rule League Member for County Meath in 1875. He subsequently sat for the constituency of Youghal, Cork from 1880 until 1891.

In Parliament, Parnell participated in a policy of obstructionism for the purpose of forcing the House to deal with Irish issues. In 1877, he was elected to the presidency of the Home Rule Confederation of Great Britain. In 1879, with Michael Davitt, he spoke in front of a massive tenants' meeting in Westport, County, Mayo, stating: "You must show the landlord that you intend to keep a firm grip on your homesteads and lands. You must not allow yourselves be dispossessed as you were dispossessed in 1847." His speech became the first salvo in the Land War.

After the 1880 general election, Parnell became the leader of the new Home Rule League party. Together with his party lieutenants, Parnell was arrested in October 1881 under The Coercion Act for "sabotaging the Land Act." From Kilmainham Jail, he issued the "No Rent Manifesto," calling for tenant farmers to refuse to pay their rents. The Land League was immediately suppressed.

In March and April 1887, Parnell was accused by the *Times* of supporting the Phoenix Park murders. After letters were published suggesting that Parnell had been complicit in the murders, he requested a Commission of Enquiry. In February 1889, the letters were shown to be forgeries written by Richard Piggott, a disgruntled former Parnell supporter, and Parnell was vindicated.

During the period 1886–90, Parnell continued to pursue Home Rule with the support of Prime Minister Gladstone. However, on December 24, 1889, Captain William O'Shea filed for divorce from his wife, citing Parnell as co-respondent. A two-day trial revealed that Parnell had been the long-time lover of Katherine O'Shea and had fathered three of her children, creating a huge public scandal. A divorce decree was granted, but

Parnell's two surviving children with Katherine were placed in William O'Shea's custody.

Although the Irish National League passed a resolution confirming Parnell's leadership, the hierarchy of the Catholic Church in Ireland was shocked by Parnell's adultery and feared that he would wreck the cause of Home Rule. Gladstone warned that if Parnell retained the leadership, it would mean the loss of the next election as well as the end of their alliance. Parnell dug in, and the alliance collapsed. A greatly weakened party divided into Parnellite and anti-Parnellite factions.

Parnell died in his home in Hove, Devon, on October 6, 1891 of pneumonia with his wife, Katherine, by his side. His funeral was held at Glasnevin Cemetery in Dublin and was attended by more than 200,000 people. (Compiled from Wikipedia: "Charles Stewart Parnell")

Parnell, Anna and Fanny – Sisters of Charles Stewart Parnell who founded the Ladies Land League (the LLL). The women held public meetings and encouraged country women to be active in withholding rent, boycotting, and resisting evictions. They raised funds for the Land League and for the support of prisoners and their families and distributed Land League wooden huts to shelter evicted tenant families. By the beginning of 1882, the LLL had 500 branches and thousands of women members and distributed £60,000 in relief aid, leaving the LLL deeply in debt. In accordance with previous arrangements, Anna asked her brother to settle the debts. Charles agreed on the condition that the LLL be disbanded. Anna agreed. However, Charles's heavy-handedness in the dissolution of the LLL in 1882 caused a permanent rift between the siblings. (Compiled from Wikipedia: "Anna and Fanny Parnell" and *Petticoat Rebellion, The Anna Parnell Story*, Mercer Press, Dublin 2009)

Redpath, James (1833-1891) – James Redpath was an influential American publisher and writer. In 1868, he founded the Boston Lyceum Bureau that supplied speakers for lyceums throughout the country, including Mark Twain, Julia Ward Howe, Ralph Waldo Emerson, Susan B. Anthony, and Frederick Douglass. In 1880-81, he reported on the famine and land war in the West of Ireland. Redpath was deeply affected by the extreme poverty of much of rural Ireland and became an outspoken proponent of the Land League and Charles Stewart Parnell. (Wikipedia: "James Redpath") Upon his return to the United States, he published "Talks about Ireland" and *Redpath's Weekly*, both devoted to Irish causes, in which he compared Irish landlordism to the Ku Klux Clan: "Irish landlord power is the exact counterpart of American Ku-Kluxism—only it is Ku-Kluxism codified and sanctioned by law, and enforced, not by disguised bands of midnight marauders, but by disciplined detachments of the Royal Constabulary." John R. McKivigan, *Forgotten Firebrand, James Redpath and the Making of Nineteenth-Century, America*, Cornell University Press, 2008.

Shiels, Neil, Doaghmore – One of Lord Leitrim's assassins who hit Leitrim with the butt of a muzzle-loading gun. He was never arrested for Leitrim's murder and died in 1921.

Spencer, John Poyntz, 5th Earl Spencer (1835-1910) – In 1868, Spencer was made Lord Lieutenant of Ireland. He immediately had to deal with the 1869 act disestablishing the Church of Ireland, and in 1870, the new Land Act, both of which he strongly supported. Spencer, in fact, went further than most of his ministerial colleagues, including Gladstone, in arguing for the establishment of government tribunals to enforce fair rents on Irish landlords. But it was also Spencer who refused petitions asking for mercy for Patrick Higgins and Myles Joyce.

Sweeney, Patrick – Herdsman for Lord Mountmorres. Although Sweeney was repeatedly taken into custody for questioning, he was never formally charged with Mountmorres's murder. An informer testified before the Parnell Commission that Sweeney was a member of a secret ribbon society and one of several men who had participated in the assassination of the viscount.

Sources

Introduction

"Heath, bog, and rock prevail everywhere…" – George Fletcher, Editor, "Connaught," Cambridge University Press, 1922.

"Less than 800 households…" R. F. Foster, Allen Lane, *Modern Ireland 1600-1972*, Penguin Press, London, 1988.

"Nest of assassins, the breeding ground of assassination…" – "The Appalling Tragedy at Cong," *Guardian*, August 21, 1882.

Chapter 1
Vigilante Justice in Donegal

"Why don't they go after the big 'uns…" – "The Murder of Lord Leitrim," *New York Times*, April 4, 1878.

"As he rose in riches, he fell in reputation…" – *New York Times*, "Murder of Lord Leitrim," April 4, 1878.

Lord Leitrim's Letter – "Ireland," *Times* (London), December 10, 1863.

"Paid his rent regularly…" – "Ireland," *Times* (London), October 19, 1864.

"Did Lord Leitrim not bear the reputation…" – "The Stuff Some Irish Landlords Are Made Of," *Donahoe's Monthly Journal*, Vol. V. Boston: T.B. Noonan and Company, 1881.

"Punished with eviction every show of opposition..." – *Waterford News*, Waterford, Ireland, April 12, 1878, reprinting a quote from the *Londonderry Standard*.

"There were two cars in the party. The first was the Milford Hotel coach…" – Slevin, Fiona, "Lord Leitrim assassinated." *Lough Rynn*. Blog. Web

"On the evening of the day on which the murder took place, Milford..." – "Surveying in Donegal," St. Martin's-le-grande, Volume 1, *The Post Office Magazine,* October 1890 to July 1891, W. P. Griffith & Sons, Limited, Prujean Square, Old Bailey, E.C.

"The mob wanted to wreak their drunken rage on the dead body of the old Earl..." – *New York Tribune,* April 12, 1878.

"Eleven men were arrested for the crime but eight were soon discharged..." "The Killing of Lord Leitrim – County Donegal, 1878," *Donegal Generations,* September 27, 2013. Blog. Web.

"The Coal Porters' Band, followed by a dense crowd..." – "The Murder of Lord Leitrim," *Guardian,* February 24, 1879.

"Find nothing to seize. So great was the defaulter's poverty..." – "The Leitrim Estates," *Times* (London), June 3, 1879.

Chapter 3
Mini-Famine: 1877 – 1879
A Turning Point

"The poorest return ever obtained from the potato crop..." – "International Migrations," Volume II, "Irish Emigration," D.A.E. Harkness, Queen's University, Belfast, 1931.

James Hack Tuke – A Memoir, Compiled by the Right Hon. Sir Edward Fry, Macmillan and Co., Ltd., New York, 1899.

"The Irish mini famine of 1877-1879 caused hunger rather than mass starvation..." – Wikipedia, "The Irish Mini Famine."

"The Irish peasants concluded that a potato crop failure was likely to lead to famine..." – Walter Wilson Jennings, "The Irish National Land League – 1879-1881," University of Illinois Library, 1915.

Chapter 4 - The Land League

"A fair rent is a rent the tenant can reasonably afford to pay according to the times..." – "The Irish Agitator in Parliament and on the Platform," *A Complete History of Irish Politics for the Year 1879,* Philip H. Bagenal, Barrister at Law, Hodges, Foster, and Figgis, 1880. Web.

"In 1879-1882, Irish Americans publicly remitted over $5 million…" – Walter Wilson Jennings, "The Irish National Land League – 1879-1881," University of Illinois Library, 1915.

"The valuation was calculated at a time when prices were abnormally low…" – R. F. Foster, Allen Lane, *Modern Ireland 1600-1972*, Penguin Press, London, 1988.

Chapter 5
The Land War (1879-1882)

"In the collision which took place on Saturday at Knockrichard, County Mayo…" – "Ireland – Disturbances" – *New York Herald* Bureau, London, January 12, 1879.

"This was the third large demonstration held in the area…" – Parnell Commission, "The Land League and Crime," Chapter IV, 1888.

"On the 22nd September, 1880, Captain Boycott's walls…" – Parnell Commission, "The Land League and Crime," Chapter IV, 1888.

Chapter 6
Murder of Lord Mountmorres
September 25, 1880

"…prime favorite with the peasants" and "devoted himself to the amateur practice of medicine…"" "A Queer Picture of a Poor Peer's Life and Death in Ireland." – *Times-Picayune*, New Orleans, November 3, 1880.

Lack of a police escort – "The Murder of Lord Mountmorres," *Guardian*, September 29, 1880.

"…whose dress betrayed no symptom of care or neatness…" – "The Murder of Lord Mountmorres," *Guardian*, September 29, 1880.

All quotes made by James Redpath are from "Ireland's Misery," *Inter Ocean* (Chicago), October 25, 1880.

"Lord Mountmorres had a very small property and could not afford like other landlords…" – "The Murder of Lord Mountmorres," *Times* (London), September 28, 1880.

"In all complaints at the suit of the police or other authorities he was looked upon as the people's magistrate…" – "A Queer Picture of a Poor Peer's Life and Death in Ireland," *Times-Picayune,* New Orleans, November 3, 1880.

"As a magistrate he was a ferocious partisan…." – "The Stuff Some Irish Landlords Are Made Of," *Donahoe's Monthly Journal,* Vol. V., Boston: T. B. Noonan and Company, 1881.

"Lord Mountmorres was reviled as an informer, and the peasants took a dislike to him…" – "A Queer Picture of a Poor Peer's Life and Death in Ireland," *Times-Picayune,* New Orleans, November 3, 1880.

"…on Saturday he had been in Clonbur…"– "The Murder of Lord Mountmorres," *Guardian,* September 29, 1880.

"I could have believed that Sweeney would have been capable of murdering him with a stick…" – "The Murder of Lord Mountmorres," *Times,* September 30, 1880.

"The fate of Lord Mountmorres was only what bad landlords…" – *Times* (London), October 7, 1880.

"…in compliance with the order of a secret society…" – *New York Sun,* December 31, 1880.

"Witness [David Corbett] lived about a quarter of a mile beyond Ebor Hall…" – "The Murder of Lord Mountmorres," *Guardian* (London), January 27, 1881.

"By June 1880, Parnell and Davitt were to admit that they had 'lost Mayo' as Secret Societies…" – Jarlath Waldron, *Maamtrasna – The Murders and the Mystery,* Edmund Burke Publisher, Dublin, 1992.

"…excited feelings of alarm little short of actual panic among all the respectable classes…" – *Times* (London), September 28, 1880.

"Our esteemed contemporaries of the English press…view with feelings of the profoundest…" – "Murder of Lord Mountmorres," *Brooklyn Daily Eagle,* September 29, 1880.

Chapter 7
Arthur Guinness, 1ˢᵗ Baron Ardilaun

"Between 1849 and 1857, there were approximately 3,000 estates…" – "History of Ireland – Encumbered Estates Act." Web.

"Lord Ardilaun encountered the same difficulties as other landlords who have endeavoured to increase…" - Finlay Dun, "Landlords and Tenants in Ireland," Longmans, Green, and Co., London 1881.

He "organized a little bodyguard of his own people in preference to being followed…" – *Chicago Daily Tribune*, November 20, 1880.

"A caretaker of Lord Ardilaun named Cartwright discovered last night…" – *Morning News* (Belfast), December 20, 1883.

"He treated his tenants kindly, had not pressed for rent…" – "The Double Murder at Lough Mask," *Guardian* (London), January 31, 1882.

"…the inequality of the struggle in Ireland, to murder and terrorism on one side…" – "Hysterics," *Detroit Free Press*, December 9, 1881.

Chapter 8
Murders of Joseph and John Huddy

"…who wore a Caroline hat, a brown frieze coat…" and "It was after the famine years that he made his name as a bailiff. [DeBurgh] D'Arcy of Houndswood was broke…" – Katherine Tynan, *The Middle Years*, Constable and Company, London, 1917.

"John Huddy swore to tracing the footprints of his father…" – "The Lough Marks Murder Case," *Morning News* (Belfast), September 25, 1882.

"The people in the district are chiefly an Irish-speaking population…" – *Dublin Express* as reprinted in the *Guardian* (London), January 30, 1882.

"A grappling iron caught upon something weighty, which on being brought…" – "The State of Ireland, The Murder of the Two Bailiffs," *Guardian* (London), February 3, 1882.

The suspects were "conveyed the same night on cars to Galway [Jail] under a strong police escort." – *Freeman's Journal*, "The Lough Mask Tragedy," February 2, 1882.

"It was not without some difficulty that the bodies were lifted into the boat…" – "The State of Ireland, The Discovery of the Bodies of the Missing Bailiffs," *Guardian* (London), January 30, 1882.

"As an instance of the feeling existing in the locality…" – "Compensation Act," *Daily Express*, December 28, 1882.

"The Crown Solicitor based his application for a remand…" – *Guardian* (London), February 9, 1882.

"…did not deem it expedient to proceed with the charge…" – *Guardian* (London), February 23, 1882.

"Always accompanied by eight or more of the tallest, beefiest RIC…" – *Maamtrasna*, p. 31.

"Kerrigan began to fear the evidence we [the Crown] had procured…" – George Bolton, *A Short Account of the Discovery and Conviction of the*

"…so demoralized by fear owing to the recent outrages…" – Finnegan, *Loughrea*, p. 133.

'Invincibles,' Some Trials of which the Writer Had Charge in 1881, 1882, 1883, and 1884," Dublin: Hodges, Figgis, and Co., 1887.

"I apprehend from my perusal of the depositions… - "Murder Trials at the Commission," *Guardian*, December 6, 1882.

Chapter 9
Maamtrasna Massacre and Phoenix Park Murders

Attack on Michael Joyce – "I asked Michael, through Sub-constable Lenihan who spoke Irish, what had happened…" – *Maamtrasna.*, p. 15.

"…a small farmer holding…six pounds worth of land…" – *Daily Express*, August 21, 1882.

"Judge Barry, in his charge to the jury, said that the discrepancy as to the number of participants in the murders was proof…" *Maamtrasna*, p. 234.

"…such a huge wrong could not continue [and] saw a probability of these men coming back to their wives…" and "It may be well for persons of noble sentiment and high mental culture…"*Maamtrasna*, p. 129.

"Lives had been taken and…innocent people had suffered…" – *Maamtrasna*, p. 155.

"There is a local tradition of a meeting held, prior to the murder…" – *Maamtrasna*, p. 313.

Chapter 10
First Trial of Patrick Higgins

"…shabby, threadbare suit of grey frieze, and his coat..." – "The Lough Mask Murders, Opening of the Trials," *Guardian* (London), December 8, 1882.

Route of process servers and "Both men were found…to have been assassinated by pistol…" – "The Lough Mask Murders – Patrick Higgins on Trial," *Morning News* (Belfast), December 8, 1882.

"On the 3rd of January, I saw Joe Huddy and a boy with him…" – "The Lough Mask Murders – Patrick Higgins on Trial," *Morning News* (Belfast), December 8, 1882.

"No more than any man in this court…" – "Ireland," *Times* (London), December 8, 1882.

"They were right over the boy murdering him with shots…" and "After breakfast on that morning, Patrick Mannion…" – "Lough Mask Murders – Patrick Higgins on Trial," *Morning News*, (Belfast), December 8, 1882.

"…fell on him and tripped him. He pulled him after him on the road." – "The Lough Mask Murders, Trial of the First Prisoner," *Dublin Daily Express*, December 8 and December 19, 1882.

"She was drawing corn [oats] with her father on that day from early in the morning…" – "Ireland," *Times* (London), December 9, 1882.

The testimony of Kate Higgins and Mary Conroy and the instructions by Judge O'Brien to the jury appeared in "Ireland," *Times* (London), December 9, 1882.

"Although the witnesses for the defence had left the table [the raised platform] somewhat under a cloud…" and "Having referred in detail to the several notices found on the body…" and "This was the last day…" – "Ireland," *Times* (London), December 11, 1882.

Teeling insisted that Kerrigan "was a leading member of the Land League in its most advanced state..." – "Ireland," *Times* (London), December 9, 1882.

Judge O'Brien's instructions to the jury: "It was plain that this was not a crime arising out of sudden provocation..." – "Ireland," *Times* (London), December 9, 1882.

"The evidence of John Haloran [sic] pointed clearly to assistance being forthcoming..." – "Lough Mask Murders – The Judge's Charge," *Morning News* (Belfast), December 11, 1882.

Chapter 11
Second Trial of Patrick Higgins

"The service of an ejectment process was a recognized motive..." – "Lough Mask Murders," *Morning News* (Belfast), December 13, 1882.

"Unless Kerrigan could destroy the evidence of the service of the process..." – "The Lough Mask Murders, The Jury Return - Patrick Higgins Guilty," *Morning News* (Belfast), December 13, 1882.

"She did not think it was any harm to swear a lie..." – *Guardian*, December 14, 1882.

"...unless they were certain of his guilt as they were of their own existence..." – "Ireland," *Times* (London), December 9, 1882.

"Before God and the Virgin, I never lifted hand..." and "that Higgins was the least guilty of the three persons concerned" – "The Lough Mask Murders – The Judge's Charge," *Morning News*, (Belfast), December 14, 1882.

"The only duty of the Judge on the conclusion of the trial was simply to have pronounced sentence..." – *Times* (London), February 27, 1883.

Justice O'Brien's charge to the jury – "The Lough Mask Murders – The Judge's Charge," *Morning News*, (Belfast), December 14, 1882.

Chapter 12
Trial of Thomas Higgins

"Kerrigan was in his barn when he saw the two Huddys coming up the boreen..." – "The Lough Mask Murders – Trial of Thomas Higgins," *Morning News* (Belfast), December 15, 1882.

"All this pointed very strongly to some influence being exercised over the young woman Laffy..." – "The Lough Mask Murders – The Judge's Charge – Verdict and Sentence," *Morning News* (Belfast), December 18, 1882.

"Mathias Kerrigan had the strongest motive..." – "The Lough Mask Murders," *Morning News* (Belfast), December 16, 1882.

Teeling's cross-examination of Kerrigan – "The Lough Mask Murders – The Judge's Charge – Verdict and Sentence," *Morning News* (Belfast), December 18, 1882.

"The jury would have to ask themselves why Mannion should have selected the prisoner Thomas Higgins..." and "I have a few words to say. On my oath..." – "The Lough Mask Murders – The Judge's Charge – Verdict and Sentence," *Morning News* (Belfast), December 18, 1882.

Chapter 13
Trial of Michael Flynn

"Michael Flynn...an elderly man, slight in stature, and more impoverished-looking..." – "The Lough Mask Murders – Trial of Michael Flynn," *Morning News* (Belfast), December 19, 1882.

"...the prisoner was seen in the boreen at Kerrigan's house..." and "leading man in the neighbourhood, who corresponded with [the Land League] on agrarian subjects..." – "The Lough Mask Murders – Trial of Michael Flynn," *Morning News* (Belfast), December 19, 1882.

"...just the sort of man to be found patrolling the boreen before the murder..." and "Michael Flynn, you have been found guilty by the jury of this crime..." – "The Lough Mask Murders – Trial of Michael Flynn," *Morning News* (Belfast), December 19, 1882.

"...to decide upon the guilt or innocence of this man as if they now first heard of the murder of the Huddys..." and "...was just the man whom they would expect to have intelligence..." – "The Lough Mask Murders – The Defence of Michael Flynn," *Morning News* (Belfast), December 20, 1882.

"On the day of Joe Joyce's funeral, I got up at day [dawn]... -- "The Lough Mask Murders – The Defence of Michael Flynn," *Morning News* (Belfast), December 20, 1882.

"I was engaged coffining Joe Joyce's remains, and on that morning, saw the prisoner Michael Flynn standing at the gable..." – "The Lough Mask Murders – The Defence of Michael Flynn," *Morning News* (Belfast), December 20, 1882.

"...went there on the morning of the funeral. I was there when the funeral started..." and "In the evening a stranger whom she had never saw came in..." – "The Lough Mask Murders – The Defence of Michael Flynn," *Morning News* (Belfast), December 20, 1882.

"Fair and honest, I am as innocent of that crime as any man of the jury or of the Court..." – "The Lough Mask Murders – Trial of Michael Flynn – The Judge's Charge – Verdict and Sentence," *Morning News* (Belfast), December 21, 1882.

Michael Flynn's Confession: "It is stated that Michael Flynn, one of the two men who are to be executed on Wednesday for the murder of the Huddys, has made a detailed statement of his connection with the crime. He admits his own guilt, and declared the innocence of the Kerrigan family, but denies that they could have witnessed the occurrences they swore at the trial." "The Lough Mask Murders – Confession by Flynn," *Morning News* (Belfast), January 26, 1883

Chapter 14
The Queen's Justice in Galway

"There were parts of Ireland where the queen's writ no longer ran..." – Kerby Miller, *Emigrants and Exiles*, Oxford University Press, 1985.

"Cases were most commonly moved from the West and South, where the agitation was strongest..." – "The Politics of Jury Trials in Nineteenth-Century Ireland," 2015, Comparative Legal History, Niamh Howlin, Lecturer, Sutherland School of Law, University College, Dublin.

Justice O'Brien's background: *Law Times, The Journal and Record of the Law and Lawyers,* Volume 108, November 1899, and Maurice Healy, *The Old Munster Circuit,* p. 16.

Sentencing of Thomas Higgins – "Lough Mask Murders – No Reprieve," *Morning News* (Belfast), January 15, 1883 and "The Lough Mask Murders – Confession by Flynn," *Morning News* (Belfast), January 16, 1883.

Chapter 15
Questions about the Huddy Murders

"…sat in front of [Kerrigan's] door though there was another down the village." – *Maamtrasna,* p. 223.

Report on Mathias Kerrigan's conversation with Mr. Burke, Lord Ardilaun's agent: "…a process of ejectment would be issued… – "Ireland, The Lough Mask Murders," *Guardian,* December 9, 1982.

Mary Kerrigan's interview with R.M. Brady – "The Lough Mask Tragedy," *Freeman's Journal,* September 26, 1882.

"If the Virgin Mother of the God-born Child…" – "The Lough Mask Murders," *Dublin Daily Express,* December 9, 1882.

"[Mathias] Kerrigan has since gone to the bar of a higher tribunal…"– "Trial and Sequel," July 24, 1904.

Chapter 16
Aftermath

"She positioned herself at the western end of the salmon weir bridge…" – *Maamtrasna,* p. 155.

"It appears that a barrister named Edward Ennis, a frequent visitor to Green St. Courthouse…" – *Maamtrasna,* p. 179.

Epilogue

"The state paid £800,000 rent for 130,000 tenants…" – Laurence Marley, *Michael Davitt, Freelance Radical and Frondeur,* Four Courts Press, 2007.

Appendix A
Maamtrasna Massacre

They "were mountaineers of the district, dressed in the white, frieze flannel [undyed sheep's wool] which the peasantry usually wore…" – "The Appalling Tragedy at Cong," *Guardian*, August 21, 1882.

Appendix D
Lord Ardilaun after the Lough Mask Murders

"Lord Ardilaun encountered the same difficulties as other landlords who have endeavoured to increase the size…" and "He had lived among his people as much as he could…"– "Estates and Farming in South Mayo," *Times* (London), April 13, 1881.

"…every class may continue to live together in Ireland…" – *Times* (London), November 17, 1890.

"…pressed for arrears of rent. These arrears originally amounted to £23,000…" – *Daily Herald*, Delphos, Ohio, February 24, 1882.

Other books by Mary Lydon Simonsen

Non-fiction
The Mud Run Train Wreck (1888)
A Disaster in the Irish-American Community
minookamemories.blogspot.com

The Patrick Shea Mystery Series:
Three's A Crowd

A Killing in Kensington

A Death in Hampden

Dying to Write

Murder by Moonlighting
An Incident in Longmere

Printed in Great Britain
by Amazon